"Jerome is natural born brand advocator, combine that with his quick wit and sharp observations, he is able to deliver brand consultancy and training that is not only insightful, practical but more importantly, relevant and pragmatic to implement.

I consider it an honour to have worked with Jerome on several internal and external branding projects, his broad perspective on branding issues often comes in handy during our strategic branding discussions. I am looking forward to working with Jerome and his team again soon, as it was equally an enriching experience for me. "

- Michael Lim
Industry Teams Global Communications, ***BASF SE***

"Jerome is amongst one of THE most passionate individuals I have met on branding. We worked with him to conduct our internal brand engagement for our rebranding. He infected us with his energy, enthusiasm and 5Cs, which he did successfully. Now all employees of Senaat believe in the 5Cs and how to deliver our brand values consistently through all our touch points"

- Mubarak Al Ameri
Vice President - Corporate Communications, **Senaat***, Abu Dhabi, UAE*

"Jerome is a true joy to work with, his passion in Branding is exceedingly contagious. Insightful and candid, Jerome brings with him a wealth of experience, injecting fresh perspectives by integrating branding into business strategy and success. This book is a must-read for business leaders, marketers and HR professionals seeking to build truly iconic global brands."

- Samuel Teo
General Manager, **Aventis School of Management***, Singapore*

"When it comes to internal branding, Jerome Joseph wrote the book... Oh yeah, my testimonial is here on the book. Seriously, if you want to have a workforce that understands your brand, as well as attracting and retaining good employees in order to become a company of choice, you need to read this book!"

- Scott Friedman
Author, "Celebrate! Lessons Learned from the World's Most Admired Organizations"

"Jerome Joseph is nothing short of brilliant. He's a unique combination of intellectual insight on the subject of branding and a platform personality of the highest caliber. I enthusiastically recommend Jerome -- you and your organization will be richer for the experience!"

- Scott McKain
Author, "Collapse of Distinction: Stand out and move up while your competition fails"

"Virtually everyone In marketing, PR, advertising and even graphic design now claims to be a "branding" expert, but Jerome Joseph truly is. He lives and breathes brand strategy. As a colleague in the field, and fellow branding speaker based in America, I admire the research and in-depth work Jerome has done in the field."

- David Avrin
Author,"It's Not Who You Know, It's Who Knows You!"

Published by The Brand Theatre Pte Ltd

Internal Branding - Growing your Brand from Within
ISBN: 978-981-07-4111-2
Printed in Singapore

The information presented herein represents the views of the author as of the date of publication. This book is presented for informational purposes only. Due to the rate at which conditions change, the author reserves the right to alter and update his opinions at any time. While every attempt has been made to verify the information in this book, the author does not assume any responsibility for errors, inaccuracies, or omissions.

Special Acknowledgements:
- Julienne Guilles, Art Director, The Brand Theatre Pte Ltd (design/layout)
- Arnold Hozana, Customer Engagement Manager, The Brand Theatre Pte Ltd (research/template development)
- Adna Kapic (content editing)

INTERNAL BRANDING

GROWING YOUR BRAND FROM WITHIN

JEROME JOSEPH

Brand Coach & Internal Brand Strategist

CONTENTS

This book is dedicated to the loving memory of my late Grandmother, Mary Joseph, who has always been my inspiration and guide in life.

Love you Grandma!

INTRODUCTION

This book is about internal branding, and how an effective internal branding programme can help your enterprise grow and move forward in today's competitive economy.

For many readers, the concept may be unfamiliar. To understand internal branding, let's start with something that's very familiar: external branding. These are the outward features and qualities that allow consumers to quickly differentiate your product or service from your competitors. They include things like your logo, letterhead, the shape of your product container, a slogan, or a proprietary ingredient.

When you see the silhouette of a Coke bottle, you instantly know what it is. When you hear the distinctive five-note McDonald's jingle, you know it's McDonald's. When you see a passenger jet with a red tail fin, it's a Virgin jet. When a big brown truck pulls up outside your office, you know it's the UPS delivery van. These are examples of external branding.

Internal branding is a lot deeper. It's how your company is operated in relation to your customers. It's your reputation for customer service and integrity, and the quality of the brand experience that you deliver. It's your vision, mission statement and values. It's about everything your employees do, from the boardroom to the mailroom. It's the culture of your brand and an expression of what your brand stands for in every aspect of your business.

You might say that external branding attracts your customers, while internal branding keeps them. And everyone knows that long-term customers, the ones who are loyal and devoted to your brand, provide you with a steady revenue stream and a solid platform for growth.

The key to internal branding is your people and how they translate your brand. They are the ones who live it every day and convey your company's values to your customers.
This book covers the essentials of internal branding. It is your companion that will tell you what you need to know and guide you through the steps you need to take to ensure that your internal brand strategy gets all your staff on the same page.

We'll take you on a journey and bring into play our proprietary 6-Step Internal Brand Strategy Action Plan. Whether you've been working in the same company for a long time or have a new start-up, you'll gain a better understanding of your brand. By being clear about your brand yourself, you can take your team on the journey as well.

The 6-Step Internal Brand Strategy Action Plan

1 Brand Research

2 Strategic Blueprint - Brand DNA

3 Motivation and Internal Training

4 Communicate: Delivering the Experience

5 Support Systems

6 Brand Performance Measurement

Part One will help you to understand why internal branding is so important. It will teach you the importance of your employees' willingness to provide an excellent customer experience and the impact they have on your company's overall performance. Part Two will focus on what internal branding is about. After carefully studying the five Cs of internal branding you'll be prepared to take the step towards an aligned internal brand. No worries, we will not leave you with just the why and the what, but also the how. Part Three introduces the 6-Step Internal Brand Strategy Action Plan (IBSAP) and shows you step by step how you will get your employees aligned and a strong internal brand implemented.

You'll find fascinating case studies of world-class brands including Southwest Airlines, Google, Starbucks, Apple, Disney, and many more. At the end of each chapter you'll find the key insights to remember and quick exercises to help you apply the know-how to your own company.

Finally, when you set off on your brand journey, be ready to go the extra mile with a bonus chapter on creating a Branded Culture using Brand Associations and Dynamic Stories.

Ready?

Fasten your seatbelt and let's start your journey!

PART 1: WHY?

> Let one who wants to move and convince others, first be convinced and moved themselves. If a person speaks with genuine earnestness the thoughts, the emotion and the actual condition of their own heart, others will listen because we all are knit together by the tie of sympathy.
>
> ***Thomas Carlyle,***
> *Scottish writer and satirist*

Chapter 1:

THE BEGINNING: YOUR BRAND IS YOUR PROMISE

To be profitable, a business needs to grow. Steady growth can be achieved only when the enterprise differentiates itself from its competition. With global communication, easy access to the Internet, and greater opportunities to do business, the market has become bigger. That's great news, but on the flip side, the market is also much more crowded, and that means it's a lot more challenging to get noticed. A quick search on the Internet is enough to tell you there may be thousands of companies competing in your market segment.

To stand out from the crowd, you need to be doing things differently. That's where branding comes in. One of the most powerful sources of competitive differentiation, branding gives you the opportunity to send a clear message to your customers about who you are, what you do, and perhaps most importantly, what they'll experience when they do business with you. In other words, the customer and the overall brand experience will become targeted, differentiated, and predictable. This in turn drives customer loyalty.

Another way you can differentiate yourself is by not making the same mistake made by so many businesses that get into branding. They invest heavily to establish their brand, plan their branding statements, print their collaterals to deliver their brand message, set up their website and write their brand stories. Everything is set up to succeed until the last hurdle – they forget to tell their staff!

You've often heard companies assert that their staff are their greatest assets. Perhaps that claim has become a bit clichéd. Nevertheless, when it comes to branding, a truer cliché could not be found.

Your staff are the deliverers of your brand. They are your brand champions, your ambassadors and your face. It is through your staff, and often your staff alone, that your brand is communicated at each and every customer touch point – that crucial make-or-break encounter between the customer and your business. At every single customer touch point your brand must find its mark without fail!

For there is no point investing in establishing a strong brand identity if your customers don't get to experience it because your staff:

- Don't know about it (it happens!)
- Don't understand it
- Don't care about it
- Aren't motivated to deliver it

It's like inviting people to your party and then forgetting to tell them the address, or investing in a fantastic website that no-one can find, or creating the perfect home and neglecting to buy insurance.

When you put all that expense and effort into creating your brand, you need to ensure that your staff can and will deliver the brand to your customer. You need to get your organisation aligned and focused on the inside to deliver on your brand promise. You need to ensure that everyone is on the same page.

This is where internal branding comes in. Internal branding has become one of the most important aspects of a company's branding strategy. It is essentially branding from the inside out, and is widely practised globally in world-class organisations.

Internal branding sets up systems for you to educate your staff on what your brand stands for, to train them to deliver your brand at all touch points, so that they deliver a truly branded experience that reflects the values and key branding elements of your organisation. Internal branding gives you that differentiation. If you implement your internal branding strategy correctly, it becomes a dynamic evolutionary force that will promote your brand more effectively than any advertising campaign.

With such a strategic force behind you, you will have a brand that will work for you, as long as it comes from the inside out, and as long as it begins with internal branding.

This is a positive step forward, but just how do you implement it? How do you get the totality of your organisation to understand and care about your brand promise? And having done that, how do you get your organisation to deliver that promise across all touchpoints?

Your solution is to create an internal brand-building culture across your organisation, because until everyone in your organisation, from the CEO to the latest intern, can accurately and consistently articulate your brand promise, all your efforts to promote your brand externally will have come to nothing.

So what do we mean by "brand promise"? Well, your brand is a promise that you make to your customers and one you must never fail to keep. You start by carefully assessing the competition and then, establishing the pledge you will make that is so distinctive, it will set you apart and give you the best competitive advantage. This is your brand promise, and it must be consistently delivered through every marketing activity, every action, every corporate decision and every customer interaction, not just externally, but internally as well. This involves ensuring that everyone in the organisation knows what the brand promise is and fully embraces it. It is only when everyone is on the same page that you'll find that politics and other self-serving agendas will eventually become less, because now everyone on-board is united in promoting the brand.

Your brand promise must do more than drive your marketing campaigns. Your total brand experience at every touch point must reinforce your brand promise to your audience. It only takes the failure of one employee to break that promise and damage your brand. Here's just one example of a brand that suffered because the organisation did not have a strong internal brand dedicated to total customer satisfaction.

The "United Breaks Guitars" Scandal

Sometimes, one customer can make a huge difference. In 2008, musician Dave Carroll's cherished Taylor guitar was broken by baggage handlers on a United Airlines flight. After the airline repeatedly declined to reimburse him for the damage, Carroll wrote the song "United Breaks Guitars", decrying their poor customer service. He posted the video on YouTube, and within weeks over ten million people had seen the clip.

The damage to United's brand was substantial; some stock analysts assert that within a week of the video being posted online, United Airline's stock price fell ten percent, representing a loss to the stockholders of about $180 million in value. How true that is remains to be seen, but the damage on the brand cannot be questioned. Imagine if ten million people read about your incompetence, and out of which one million posted similar comments? Imagine the multiple impacts on your brand. United could have spared itself this public relations humiliation if it had followed its own policy on customer service. United's website says: "In the air and on the ground, online and on the telephone, our customers have the right to expect – to demand – respect, courtesy, fairness and honesty from the airline they have selected for travel."

This is truly the age of the customer, because any customer can, in theory, do what Dave Carroll did: use talent, fight back, connect with millions of other customers, and knock hundreds of millions of dollars off the market value of a massive corporation. All it takes is one employee and one angry customer.

The above case study demonstrates how important having alignment to the internal branding is. Every employee in every department needs to get onboard what the brand stands for and ensure that it is reflected consistently.

On implementing your internal brand strategy, you are bound to face at least some of the following barriers:

- The organisation culture doesn't support the brand
- The organisation's systems don't support the brand
- The brand gets lost amidst other corporate messages
- Management not focused on the brand
- A short attention span for the brand delivery. It can start off with a bang then fizzle out as other corporate decisions take precedence
- Management doesn't quite buy into the brand
- Management is resistant to change
- Staff don't own the brand
- Too many units operating in their own silos

In order to tackle resistance to change and get everyone on the same page, you need to address all of the following and ensure they are aligned to your brand:

- Mission and vision
- Business planning process
- Corporate culture
- Recruitment
- Internal communication tools
- Training and development
- Performance objectives
- Performance appraisal
- Rewards and recognition
- Products and services
- Operations, systems and logistics

This book will help you address all of the above issues so that you keep your promise as a brand, not just to your customers, but also to all your employees.

KEY INSIGHT

Key Insights of Chapter 1

- Your brand is the key to identification and acceptance by your customers.
- Your brand promise is the implied commitment your company makes to your customers.
- Don't make the common mistake of focusing on your external brand and not involving your employees.
- Employees are your most important touchpoint to deliver your brand to your audiences.
- Your internal brand is comprehensive and affects every part of your operation.

> 20% of the brand is about things such as logo, stationery, and brochures. The other 80% is about brand behaviour through your employees.
>
> ***Jerome Joseph,***
> *CEO, The Brand Theatre*

Chapter 2:

WHY INTERNAL BRANDING IS IMPORTANT

Before we look at internal branding, let's pause for a moment and first gain a good understanding of what overall branding actually is. It is much more than a façade, an image on a shop front, or mere packaging. It's more than just your logo design or corporate colours. Branding is the life of your organisation because it defines the business behaviours, core values and customer promise.

A brand is a living entity - and it is enriched or undermined cumulatively over time, the product of a thousand small gestures.

Michael Eisner, *former CEO of Walt Disney*

This is a short quote, and yet it speaks volumes to the impact (whether positively or negatively) that the actions of your staff can have on your brand. While admittedly some people want to clock in, do a job, and cruise on home, most people truly want to be part of something bigger than them. They want to be part of a Living Breathing brand that stands for something. Earlier on, we shared the impact that one tiny gesture can have on a customer. We cannot stress again and again the criticalness of having all employees on board the brand. The combination of their gestures and alignment will create that living breathing brand!

For many companies, the temptation is to concentrate all branding efforts externally towards the customers. But an organisation is made up of people, and it is the people that drive that brand message. If you don't put systems in place to enable these important people to deliver your brand to your customers, your efforts on external branding will be for nothing. To get an idea of what we are talking about, take a look at the points below:

WHAT INTERNAL BRANDING SHOULD DO*

- **Define your world**
  Your internal brand must frame the systems that your business puts into place as well as leverage the personality of your business: its culture, identity and unique attributes.

- **Define what your business believes in**
  Your internal brand must be a collective representation of all that your business stands for, fights for and believes in.

- **Define your big picture and how this is connected to your employees**
  Your brand will define what you need your employees to believe aspirationally, inspirationally, emotionally and functionally.

- **Articulate your promises to your employees**
  Your brand is your promise to your employees to provide experience that in return will motivate their commitment to deliver your brand.

- **Simplify the people factor**
  Brand can keep a business focused on what really matters, and help establish emotional connections with the people who determine the business' destiny.

- **Create a map for "on-brand behaviour"**
  Your brand will only thrive if employees are able to translate your brand with the correct behaviours. Behaviours need to be clearly mapped out and elaborated to ensure that every employee is behaving according to the brand.

- **Define your customer experience for your employees so they can deliver it**
  Your brand will only thrive if it makes a difference to customers through the touch points of your business, delivered through your employees. Your employees will need to know exactly what is expected of them to deliver the brand effectively. The ideal way is to have your employees experience the brand for themselves as the customer, by putting them in the customer's shoes. Asking your employees questions like, "How would you feel if..." should have them feeling what the customer experience should be. They will then be better positioned to deliver that experience to the customer.

- **Define "What's in it for me?"**
  To be motivated to give of themselves, people need some kind of incentive. You're asking your employees to live up to your brand standards. Their natural demand will be "What's in it for me?" They need a purpose for what they are doing, which is why they need to be aware of the value of their contribution and the rewards expected for delivering to standard.

- **Connecting outside with inside**
  Your internal brand must connect with your employees with what happens outside to what happens inside. Your employees need to understand what it is about the internal brand that will drive them to deliver the external brand.

- **Establish your reputation as a place to work**
  Brands live inside the business. Just as you do on the outside, on the inside you experience a touch point each time you access something the business offers, hear a message the business sends, use a product or service the business delivers. As much as you need to deliver your brand promise to your external customer, you need to deliver what was promised to your employees too. Are your employees receiving a branded employee experience? Your business needs to have a reputation for being a great place to work, treating its staff well, rewarding its staff appropriately, and delivering a work/life balance to its employees.

82% of people looking for jobs online consider it very important how others perceive the company they might work for.

Yahoo Poll 2005

**Reference: Brand From the Inside: Eight Essentials to Emotionally Connect Your Employees to Your Business Libby Sartain, et al*

- **Help you recruit employees**
  Once you are clear about your internal and external branding, you will be in a much better position to be able to identify and hire people who are aligned to your brand. You will be clear on what kind of skills are required for each position to deliver the brand experience at the required touch points. If you can set out at the interview selection process and at the interview itself what you require from the potential employee, certainty of alignment is that much more concrete. The employee is also more likely to be attracted to a company that can articulate clearly what it wants and expects. This clear communication allows for a good working relationship right from the start of the employee's contract.

- **Define your desired emotional connection with your employees**
  Your internal brand provides the emotional connection with employees on the inside that allows them to connect with your customers on the outside. Your internal brand must project what an employee aspires to be by connecting with your business. It must inspire the employee to become an advocate for your business and to emotionally invest in the mission to deliver your brand promise.

- **Support your growth strategy**
  If your business strategy is based on growth, it will help you point the direction towards growth. Likewise, if your business strategy is about change it can help you build a brand centred on the message of change.

- **Increase your profits**
  The bottom line to the Internal Brand Action Strategy is that once in place, an effective internal brand will increase productivity, lower employee turnover, heighten staff motivation, and boost customer satisfaction. The net result? Your company could see a measurable increase in profits.

As you see, there are many reasons why internal branding matters. That is why you should have a clear idea of your branding strategy, including internal and external branding. Make sure you put the same effort on both sides to have a strong overall brand, created inside and delivered outside.

BALANCE BETWEEN INTERNAL AND EXTERNAL BRANDING

Mind the gap! Because if you don't, your customers could very easily get caught in the gap between the brand promise and actual experience. Even before becoming a customer, seeing a gap between what you say and what you deliver can make the customer turn around. In the end the mixed messages can have more negative than positive effects on your brand.

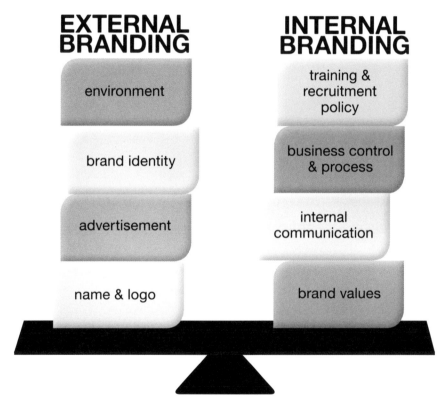

EXTERNAL BRANDING
environment
brand identity
advertisement
name & logo

INTERNAL BRANDING
training & recruitment policy
business control & process
internal communication
brand values

Clearly investing in the left hand side is pointless without paying equal attention to the properties on the right. Aligning the right with the left allows your organisation to deliver a successful brand experience.

AOL Brand Gap

Internet service provider America Online (AOL) is an example of how employee behaviour can reduce a company's brand promise. It can also be related to the tough times AOL has been going through over the last years.

First launched in 1991, at its peak in 2001 AOL had nearly 30 million subscribers. By 2009, the number had dwindled to a little over five million.

Stated on AOL's corporate website, with the commitment to create an easy access to the internet and online experience, was this pledge: "We do all these things and much more because at AOL, we are dedicated to the simple premise that our members and consumers deserve the best possible – and most valuable – online experience available anywhere."

Unfortunately, AOL's external branding was not consistent with the company's internal operations. The cited promise was clearly at odds with the experiences of customers who posted complaints at ConsumerAffairs.com. Thousands of customers were cancelling their AOL accounts, complaining about problems with AOL, rude customer service representatives, unauthorised charges and even double billing. Clearly, this was a case where the brand was not able to deliver on their promise.

THE IMPORTANCE OF KEEPING YOUR PROMISES

At the end of the day, your brand promise should define your entire business and be a guiding principle for your company's employees. At the same time, it defines what the customer can expect from the brand. So to create a successful experience between your employee and the customer, they have to talk about the same thing. The experience will not be satisfying for the customer if the employee doesn't know what the company promises outside.

You don't know what a **brand promise** is? **You're not alone.** Gallup research has found that only **40%** of employees feel that they really understand their company's brand promise.

For example, look at a retail company. If a retailer promises an "easy return policy" for their customers but at the same time penalises store managers for having too many returns, it will be hard to fulfil the brand promise and the promise will inevitably be broken. Then, when the brand fails to keep the promise, consumers become confused and dissatisfied. It will be a normal human reaction to turn away from your brand.

A BRAND IS A PROMISE AND YOU HAVE TO KEEP YOUR PROMISES!
More importantly, your EMPLOYEES have to keep your promises!

DELIVERING A SUCCESSFUL BRANDED EXPERIENCE IS THE KEY TO KEEPING YOUR BRAND PROMISE

All of the following will need to be taken into consideration when planning your Internal Branding Programme to ensure that your customers receive a total branded experience – the one you have just promised!

Experience - What you offer: How are you going to ensure that your employees will deliver the planned brand experience? You will need to consider service standards, maintenance of ambiance, maintenance of product quality, etc.

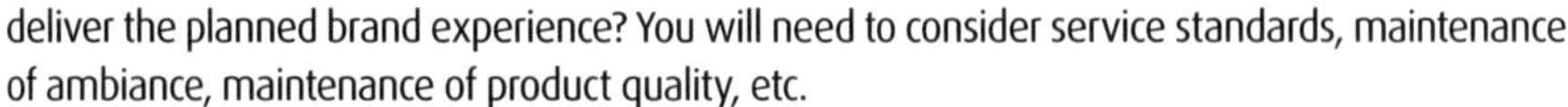

Image - How you are seen: Does the image convey your brand? Whatever your customer sees should scream your brand! You will need to consider uniforms, code of conduct, staff appearance, displays, uniformity of collaterals, brand colours and fonts, etc.

Processes and policies - What we know/do: Do your staff capabilities measure up to brand expectations? You will need to consider recruitment policies, minimum education and skills requirements for each position, regular staff training to enhance or maintain capabilities, etc.

Culture - How we behave: Is your corporate culture in line with your brand? As a multimedia design company, you would not require your creative staff to dress in business suits. Your offices would not have standard corporate décor. You would align your corporate culture with the industry you are in and the brand you have built. When your clients walk into a multimedia design company, they would not be surprised to see the employees dressed in casual wear, with trendy accessories and creative haircuts. They would expect décor that inspires creativity that might even include basketball hoops, table soccer games, bean bags strewn across the floor... you get the idea. You wouldn't demand that staff stay at their desk to work. Their line of work requires inspiration and freedom to explore ideas away from the computer and with other people. This is the corporate culture of a multimedia design company we visited and we were very impressed that their brand was reflected very clearly in their culture.

In contrast, you would want your banker to be dressed conservatively and for the office to project a professional image.

The key as we have continually stressed is for your employees to deliver the aligned brand experience, which is why we devote the entire next chapter to the importance of your employees.

CASE STUDY

Case Study: Disney

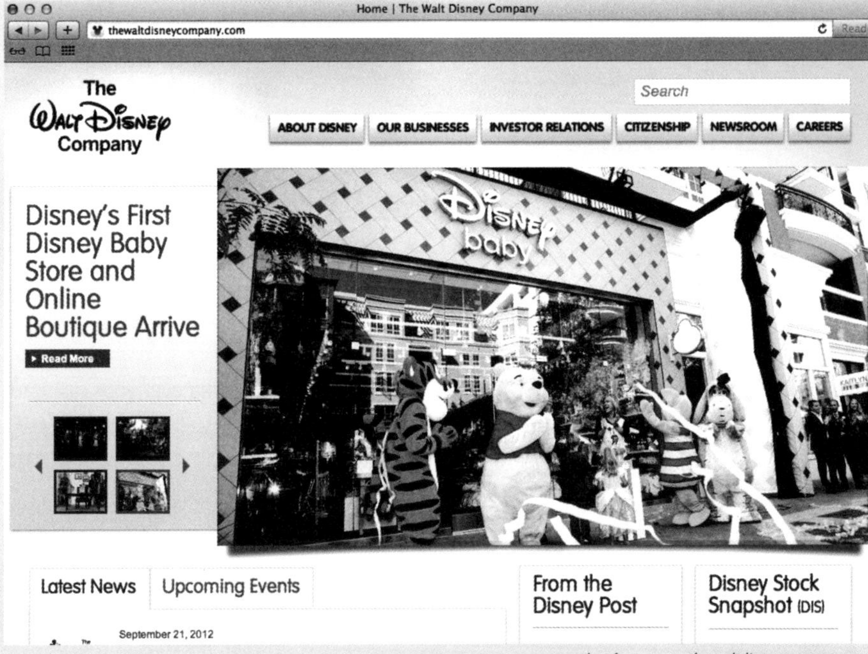

snapshot from www.thewaltdisneycompany.com

Founded in 1923 in Anaheim, California, the Walt Disney Company has achieved phenomenal success at creating a brand that blends art and science. With revenues of $40 billion a year, it is the world's largest media conglomerate.

According to its website, "The Walt Disney Company has remained faithful in its commitment to producing unparalleled entertainment experiences based on its rich legacy of quality creative content and exceptional storytelling. Today, Disney is divided into four major business segments: Studio Entertainment, Parks and Resorts, Consumer Products, and Media Networks. Each segment consists of integrated, well-connected businesses that operate in concert to maximise exposure and growth worldwide."

Astute market research, focus groups, maximising brand exposure, education, and technology are all part of Disney's brand strategy. The organisation understands what its target audience wants: wholesome family entertainment in a world of imagination, and it constantly measures and adjusts to maintain this brand.

Matthew Ryan, senior vice president and in charge of brand, franchise and customer relationship management, explains how this Disney brand influences the decisions made at the organisation.

"At some companies, responsibility for brand is assigned to the marketing department, or maybe product development. At Disney, everyone, from the CEO to interns who work in our parks, is responsible in every single decision-making moment. Long before anyone else in the media and entertainment industry had recognised the power of a strong brand, Disney had made it part of how we do business. Our front-line cast members who interact directly with the public know the importance of delivering against brand expectations. Our operations teams always think about the impact of their decisions on the products we make. Finance executives must always consider the brand impact of financial decisions. At Disney, everyone is encouraged to innovate, which sometimes means taking risks. But the risks we won't take are the ones that could jeopardise the trust that people have in our brand."

As illustrated above, Disney has been able to integrate all aspects of the branding process to create a powerful brand. Likewise, multiple aspects of your business must integrate to drive the effectiveness of your brand. Some of these aspects include:

Understanding your customer

Brands should be customer-driven and you can't affect brand perceptions of your business without understanding your customers and what it is they want. Branding experts at Disney know the company's audience very well. For example, knowing that their children are their primary audience, they make shop windows low enough that the merchandise can be seen from a stroller.

Getting it right internally

A strong brand is represented in every customer touch point. External marketing alone cannot carry a brand and will mean nothing if your brand isn't carried beyond it or the promises don't ring true on delivery. If your employees aren't happy, your customers will feel and reflect that negativity. Disney knows that keeping its employees happy and treating them well will help to ensure positive customer-employee interactions.

Walk the talk

Merely stating your values and promises isn't enough. You need to walk the talk and live up to these values. In this way, you will strengthen your brand and customer loyalty. Disney is a great example of a company that lives its values. Its worldwide outreach programme supports public service initiatives, community outreach and volunteer programmes. Disney's environmental beliefs have led to the creation of The Disney Wildlife Conservation Fund, which donates cash and makes public service announcements and encourages volunteerism globally. Disney employees volunteer their time and talents in their communities – an effort that only enhances the brand image of Disney. And the annual Enviroports (environmental report) that Disney publishes yearly keeps its shareholders in touch with how it deals with environmental issues such as reduction of waste, fossil-fuel use and greenhouse gas emissions, as well as improved eco-system protection.

Honing external communications

Every opportunity in front of your customer is an opportunity to reinforce brand and this is where careful planning of external communications to support the brand is crucial. A visit to any of the Disney properties reinforces the importance of consistently representing your brand. Employees follow strict brand guidelines from their appearance to how they speak to guests to communicate their care for children and families.

As motivation to their employees, Disney promises on its career site, "Yes, there really are dream jobs. Here, the bottom line is imagination, our culture is magic and wonder, and required previous work experience: childhood dreams." This incentivises employees to perform better and customer interactions will be stronger, enabling them to deliver the total customer experience that is driven from their brand.

KEY INSIGHT

Key Insights of Chapter 2

- An overall brand strategy should include external and internal branding and will only succeed if they are consistent.
- Internal branding is about aligning on brand -behaviour throughout your workforce.
- Internal branding will help your employees to deliver on your brand promise.
- Internal branding will establish a basis for a one-of-a-kind branded customer experience.
- Internal branding, done right, can impact the financial bottom-line of your brand, creating competitive advantage and strong brand recognition

> In a competitive world, organisations are realising that only people can brand products and services effectively – that we are not just selling a branded product but a mass of branded people who support and deliver it.

Helena Rubenstein,
Managing Director, The HR Lab, UK

Chapter 3:

KNOW THE IMPORTANCE OF YOUR EMPLOYEES

THE NEED FOR EMPLOYEE BRAND DEVELOPMENT

A positive relationship exists between employee alignment to the internal brand, and the overall performance of an organisation. Forrester Research which is an ongoing research on customer experience and its correlation with loyalty and revenue suggests again that there is a demonstrable correlation between a person's customer experience with a given company and his or her willingness to spend more money with that company. Or in other words, his or her willingness to keep spending money with that company.

How much impact was there in 2012?

Obviously, it varies by industry, but two industries in particular should be paying closer attention to this.

Forrester found that the impact of customer experience on hotels and wireless service carriers was more than $1 billion for each industry. The data is part of Forrester's report, "The Business Impact of Customer Experience, 2012." The statistics in the latest report are part of Forrester's North American Technographics Customer Experience Online Survey from the fourth quarter of 2011. The main finding, as it has been for the past several years, is that companies with higher customer experience scores tend to demonstrate and drive higher customer loyalty. They are also more likely to win recommendations from those customers, which translates into incremental revenue, the report suggested.

This principle has wildly been supported through the human resource and management practices of many well-known, successful organisations. The principle is clear. If people can provide a branded experience there is an impact on customer loyalty and this translates into higher revenue. It is likely that these companies achieve that status, partly, because their employees commit a substantial amount of their resources to strengthen the company's brand.

So how do you get there? First you have to tell your employees what the brand stands for, but what's more important is the longer process of assimilation. The employees' understanding of the branding needs to be consistently developed as everything changes with time. Imagine a company that changes its positioning or corporate mission statement without thoroughly teaching their employees. Or a new product is launched with a totally new target group. How could they possibly deliver a consistent message to customers?

But even if there aren't any major changes, it is very important to constantly align your employees to the brand. Never forget your employees are your company's greatest assets. What they say about your company and how they act in the workplace impacts on your image, your customer experience and your overall brand.

With a good training programme you can get everybody on track by equipping them with the knowledge and tools to deliver your brand. Define the behaviours aligned with your brand and hold employees accountable. Set up a performance measurement and send incentives for good performance.

This can be implemented relatively easily! Still, many managers seem to view employee training and development as more optional than essential. This viewpoint may lead to severe problems that threaten your business.

If you are still not convinced about the importance for your employees to be trained and updated on the brand's values, mission and vision, have a look at the list below. Your front line employee does so much more than operating the cashier, replying to customer emails, or ordering new products.

WHAT YOUR EMPLOYEES DO

They keep your customers!

One of the main reasons why consumers jump brands is the attitude of indifference displayed by employees.

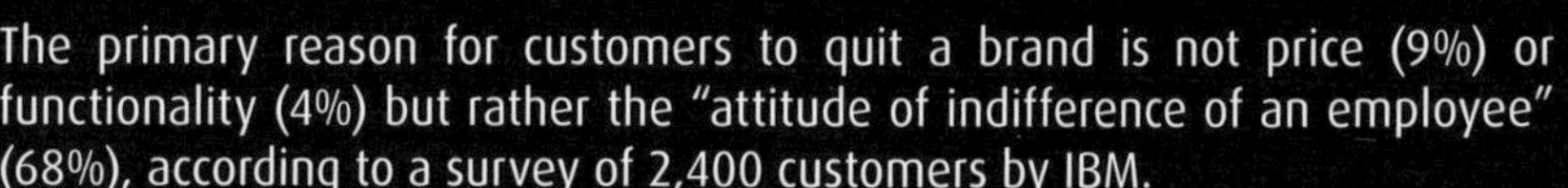

The primary reason for customers to quit a brand is not price (9%) or functionality (4%) but rather the "attitude of indifference of an employee" (68%), according to a survey of 2,400 customers by IBM.

This statistic is critical because it highlights how crucial it is that your employees drive your brand, but not drive away your customers! Every gesture counts and even a single employee can impact or damage your brand in this digital age.

Domino's Gone Bad

In 2009, a major crisis involving Domino's Pizza and its employees brought national media attention to the pizza company.

Two employees recorded themselves and put up that video on YouTube doing inappropriate and unsanitary things to the food that was being prepared for customers.

The video immediately received thousands of views and Domino's was thrown into a social media crisis. The employees were dealt with, fired, and Domino's released an official video via YouTube from the President apologising and explaining the isolated incident.

As The New York Times reported, in just a few days, Domino's reputation was damaged. The perception of its quality among consumers went from positive to negative, according to the research firm YouGov, which holds online surveys of about 1,000 consumers every day regarding hundreds of brands.

Imagine the cost to brand equity and on top of that cost in terms of time and efforts from the crisis management team to build back the image of the brand. All due to the actions of 2 employees.

WHY ARE YOUR EMPLOYEES SO IMPORTANT?

Your employees are important to your brand for several key reasons:

They can become the glue that sticks!

Think about your own experiences with a brand as a customer. You probably have a few stories of unsatisfactory service. Chances are, some of those occasions drove you away from the brand for good because most people tend to remember negative experiences more vividly than positive experiences.

They influence your customers' choices!

Your brand promises your customers a defined set of experiences at each touch point. Every time your company and your customer touch, the authenticity of your brand promise is tested. Every time your customer touches your brand through your employee, they will ask, "Am I getting what is promised?"

They define what your customer will experience!

Essentially, your brand sells on emotion, through your people. The emotional connection is at the heart of your customer's relationship with your brand. By getting your internal branding strategy correct, you will create positive emotional experience for your employee who in turn will be able to translate this in your overall brand experience.

It only takes one bad apple!

Customers have an amazing ability to store memories. It only takes one bad apple in an organisation to spoil the customer's experience of the entire brand. The customer is more likely to remember the one bad experience than the dozen good ones. It is well known that when a customer experiences good services, he will mention it to two or three people if it made that much of an impression. This is because we expect good service, and when we get it, it doesn't seem out of the norm, so it's not much of a conversation piece. However, receive bad service and you could be talking about it for weeks! How many more people will you tell? Not only will you tell your story, but you will probably warn your friends not to patronise that brand again.

To illustrate how just one bad experience can colour your customer's perception of your brand permanently, even after a prior good record, we will take the case of a bad brand experience of an advertising professional in Asia, that not only turned him away from the brand but made him an advocate for boycott of the brand. This is a lesson illustrating that your employees must be on brand in all situations they are representing the company, and not only towards immediate consumers.

The Traumatised Vendor

The advertising executive was visiting the company in question, a well-known bakery brand, to make a pitch with visuals to rebrand the company. Although the appointment had been made and the executive and his team arrived before time, the manager in-charge of branding for the bakery company failed to turn up for the meeting and had to be hunted down by her colleagues. On finally entering the room, she made no apology for being late and rudely dismissed the team's visuals and left.

This left the advertising executive understandably incensed. He had expected the same respect and professionalism he had accorded the company and was amazed at the behaviour of the branding manager. She, of all employees, should have been aware that her responsibility to the company was to carry through the company's brand messaging not just to customers but to all parties the company dealt with.

The result of this meeting was that the advertising executive swore never to shop at the brand again and spread the message to everyone he could, including on-line on several blogs. These blogs eventually got the attention of the company directors. The advertising executive received an apology, but the damage had been done – all because one employee failed to deliver the brand promise.

CASE STUDY

Case Study: Prêt a Manger

The Prêt brand is about fresh, tasty and homemade products with natural ingredients served by people who are passionate about what they do. When Prêt a Manger, which is French for "ready to eat," was launched in London in 1986 by two college friends, they aimed for proper sandwiches without the chemicals, additives and preservatives you usually find in a corner store sandwich.

But it is not only the good quality sandwiches - which would be quite easy to copy - that make Prêt such a success. It is how the company thinks about their staff. Jay Chapman from the communications department is frequently asked for the key to Pret's success. She tells that she'd love to have a scary sounding formula to impress with, but to her it's pretty simple: all about staff. She herself is passionate about employee engagement, so her "recipe" simply states, "If you treat your employees well and involve them in the decisions that will affect them, they're much more likely to be engaged in carrying out the effects of those decisions."

It's at shop level that Pret's most differentiating behaviours come into play. Firstly each team member is empowered from their first day at work to make their own decisions. If a customer comes in the store to complain about his coffee, the employee will not disappear in a back room to talk to the manager. It is up to the team member to decide how to resolve the problem. And empowerment doesn't stop there.

Says Jay Chapman, "It's not uncommon to find that if you've been in to Prêt for your lunch every day for a week, the guy behind the till will recognise you and decide to give you Friday for free. The manager keeps an eye on things, but overall the team members are empowered to make their own decisions."

Prêt invests a lot in its recruitment, training and rewarding to ensure everybody works "on-brand" for the brand.

The first step to build such a very engaged and close staff-team at each of the Prêt stores is the recruitment process, which is quite different from those of other companies. It requires prospective employees who have made it through the interview to work in a Prêt store for one day. The employees of that store then make the final decision as to whether or not the person is hired. Only a small percentage of applicants make it as a Prêt employees, but you can be relatively sure those that do, become the best brand ambassadors with the right Prêt attitude.

This process is one of many ways of empowering and inspiring existing employees at Pret. The important contribution of staff at every level, whether preparing a sandwich or pouring a coffee, is consistently acknowledged by Pret's reward and recognition programme. For example, all employees can benefit from the firm's mystery shopper scheme. Staff are put to the test when a Prêt representative, posing as an ordinary customer, drops into a shop to review the customer service. If he or she feels well served and the Prêt personality is shining through, the team will be awarded with a pay increase for the week the mystery shopper visited.

Another brand-building specialty at Prêt is their buddy system, in which its corporate managers are sent into Prêt stores so they can better familiarise themselves with the daily operation of the business. It allows office staff to keep in touch with the shop team and understand their daily work. When Esther O'Halloran, head of recruitment, spent a day at a shop for the first time, she found working behind the counter to be challenging. As head of recruitment and retention she normally isn't called upon to demonstrate her sandwich-making skills, but Prêt believes that a good knowledge of how products are made, how customers are served, and the interface between customers and Pret's service delivery system will help managers make better decisions in all aspects of the business. At the same time it serves to motivate the staff working on the shop floor.

The objective of these and many other Prêt reward and recognition programmes is to motivate employees and align them to the Prêt brand. As a result, more than 80% of all Prêt workers receive recognition rewards each week. The overall success of Prêt once again shows the importance of employees and their behaviour towards customers and the brand – and how a strong internal brand can boost the bottom line.

KEY INSIGHT

Key Insights of Chapter 3

- Employees are the greatest asset of a company and need to grow, develop and learn with the brand over time.
- Brand-Aligned employee drives the overall performance of the brand.
- They are the major influence on a customer's brand choice – most of the time a customer's decision to stay with a brand or turn away from it is made due to the employee's behaviour towards the customer.
- Frequent training will help employees to understand and then become and stay aligned with the brand.
- We can learn from Prêt a Manger how an affective awarding system will make employees work in the brand's best interest and lead to company growth.

PART 2:
WHAT?

INTRODUCTION TO INTERNAL BRANDING: THE 5 CS

> **When I hire somebody really senior, competence is the ante. They have to be really smart. But the real issue for me is, are they going to fall in love with Apple? Because if they fall in love with Apple, everything else will take care of itself.**
>
> ***Steve Jobs,*** *former CEO of Apple*

Do your employees believe in your product and the services that you offer? Are they standing 100% behind the mission of your brand? Are they living your brand?

Internal branding is when marketing starts from the inside out. It covers the strategic processes that empower employees to deliver a positive customer experience and align them with the brand. Proven to be a key factor in business and brand success, internal branding builds the bridge between business strategy and implementation. A substantial component of the bridge are the employees, working in all positions and disciplines across the company. This makes internal branding a multi-faceted journey guiding everyone company-wide in managing their personal impact on customer experience.

If you try to meet or exceed customer expectations, then whatever has been promised to customers must be lived throughout every single employee. Strong internal branding will ensure the delivery of your brand promise.

As we have stressed before, the most successful brands understand that if employees are aligned with the brand, they will deliver a consistent expression of the brand to its customers. Now we would like to go in detail about what characterises an internal branding process – what needs to be considered when taking action. Five essential key steps – the 5 Cs – are needed for success in your internal branding effort. We will give you a short introduction to the 5 Cs now, followed by a discussion of each C in the subsequent chapters.

1. **CLARITY** is the first C and the first thing to ensure about your brand. A brand stands for something and needs to be clear what that is.
2. The second C is **COMMITMENT**, which means the dedication of the employees to the brand. It is the sincere desire and drive to go the extra mile for their brand.
3. The third C is the **CONNECTION** between the brand and the employee. It underpins the importance of your employees' belief in the company brand.
4. All effort you put into your employees branding will be all without use if there is no **CONSISTENCY**, which is what the fourth C is about. When a brand is able to show consistency through their employees, in everything they do, it will result in long term brand success.
5. The last C stands for **CHAMPION**. Turn your employees into brand champions, then into brand ambassadors internally, and finally make them able to effectively deliver the brand externally.

For a successful branding effort we encourage that your internal brand follow all of the 5 Cs. With these set up, you will be prepared to reach the overall goal of internal branding to align your employees to the company to deliver the brand promise of your organisation.

Chapter 4:

1C - CLARITY

During our 2012-2013 Internal Brand Engagement Survey we discovered that while 80% of employees knew their brand from a big picture perspective, 40% of employees said they were unclear about the guidelines and how to apply their brand across key touchpoints.

Why is this significant? Because a successful internal brand strategy must bridge the gap between familiarity with the company's mission statement or values, and knowing how to translate them into everyday frontline practice. It is one thing for the company mission statement to say, "We will strive for total customer satisfaction," but it's quite another to make sure that every cashier and salesperson and customer service rep knows how to please the customer and is empowered to do so.

CLARITY AS DIFFERENTIATOR

Strong brands are clear about what they are and what they are not. In today's time where companies are extending their brands vertically or horizontally, a lot of clarity gets lost. But the brand must have its own personality and must stick to its individuality. There have been many brands that have diluted their category, and the result is confusion for the customer. A clear brand understands its overall vision and mission, its unique promises and its values. With clarity, a brand differentiates from others by its personality and places itself in a clear position. Brand clarity ensures that the right essence is communicated.

The Volvo Experience

One car brand with a strong identity is Volvo. They are not committed to building the fastest cars or the most luxurious cars – the Volvo brand clearly stands for safety and security.

We stopped at our local Volvo dealer and asked him: "What are you all about?" He replied, "That is a simple answer: We're Volvo. We are about safety." This simple clarity separates Volvo from other car brands that are trying to be everything at once. Recently we saw an ad for a car that was priced in the high-end category lending itself to a low- to midrange computer brand. That car was Lamborghini and the computer was an Asus. Why would you dilute your premium brand by associating yourself with a midrange laptop brand?

When a customer or employee is crystal clear about what a brand stands for, it is because the brand itself is clear.

Can your articulate your brand in a nutshell? Let's do a short exercise and try to define some companies. Examples: What does the Harley Davidson brand stand for? - A symbol of American freedom lived through a motorcycle.

Activity Template

What does McDonald's stand for ... in less than twenty words. You can also try Levi's, IKEA, Marlboro, Visa or other brands that come to your mind.

....

....

....

....

Now have a look at your company! Try it on yourself. In less than twenty words, explain who your company is and define your brand. Here are some examples:

We're the most stylish sushi place in Kuala Lumpur.
We're the fastest pizza delivery service in your home town.
We're the most creative manufacturer of iPhone cases in the world.

Your company:

....

....

....

....

....

....

....

....

And hopefully, the lines above are not filled with generic descriptions such as:
We're like Google, but without advertisements.
We're the flower shop in New Village.

You probably get the point. To connect with the target person it aims for, a brand has to form something special. But there are only a few moments to create that first significant speciality. Make sure it is clear what that is. A good organisation also makes its easy for the employees to communicate this specialty, internally as well as externally. Then they can spread the message to the customer.

CASE STUDY

Case Study: BASF

Headquartered in Ludwigshafen, Germany, BASF is "The Chemical Company," the global leader in the chemical industry and a strong corporate brand.

Only ten years ago, the perception of BASF as the "tape company" was quite strong, since audio and video tape was what came to people's minds when thinking about BASF. In reality, BASF is about much more, presenting a great variety of products and services from pharmaceutical to aerospace. As a result, BASF saw a strong need to work on its brand perception in order to make sure that its target groups understood what the company actually does and stands for. The company's branding approach targeted the alignment of over 17,000 employees all over the world. The challenge was to find a corporate basis for all these people from different industries and backgrounds to understand and live the BASF brand. To do so, the company developed programmes designed to align its employee pool, and promote the new brand values and the branded work attitude expected from them.

The "We Create Chemistry" campaign was born with the emphasis on creating win-win solutions in all aspects of their business from relationships to solutions. To support this change process, workshops were held in the major Asian countries, targeting the main brand multipliers like marketing and sales, human resources, and communication. The success of the campaign and the internal activation through engagement and workshops have made a big difference to the brand equity of BASF. BASF are our clients and we are glad to have been part of their internal alignment initiatives.

KEY INSIGHT

Key Insights of Chapter 4

- Clarity is a differentiator through vision and mission, unique promises and values
- Be aware: Brand clarity can easily get lost through brand extension
- You should be able to answer "What is your brand all about?" in one clear sentence.
- Make it easy for the employees to communicate a clear message, internally as well as externally.

Chapter 5:

2C - COMMITMENT

Our survey revealed that while 80% of employees felt somewhat committed to their brand, there was a gap between commitment and motivation. Out of the 80% of the committed employees, 35% were not motivated by their brand.

The implications are that these employees, whether interacting with customers on the frontlines or working behind the scenes, are not as committed to the success of the company as they should be. The result is higher employee turnover and lost revenues.

WHAT IS EMPLOYEE COMMITMENT?

There is a story about a pharmacy that launched a new product. The product was a pain-free syringe. When launched across its pharmacy stores sales were extremely poor. The CEO called in all the pharmacists. In a dramatic move, the CEO made all the pharmacists try the pain-free syringe in front of him. There was a look of horror on their faces. Finally they gathered their courage and with trembling hands injected themselves while bracing for the pain. There was none! Of course – because it was the no-pain syringe. But because they had no belief that it was painless, they could not sell it. But once they knew for themselves that there was no pain, sales increased tremendously!

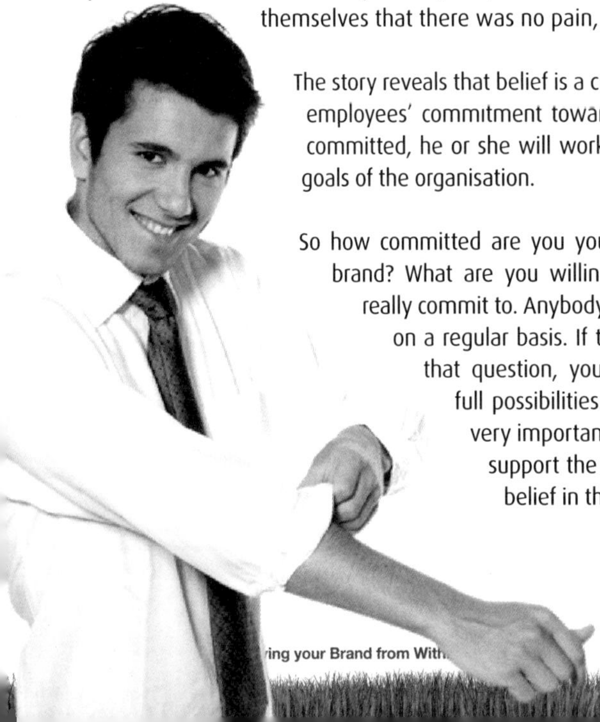

The story reveals that belief is a critical component to creating your employees' commitment towards the brand. If an employee is committed, he or she will work more effectively to support the goals of the organisation.

So how committed are you yourself to your company? To your brand? What are you willing to commit to? And we mean really commit to. Anybody should ask himself that question on a regular basis. If there is any doubt or negation to that question, you probably do not work to your full possibilities. To give a hundred percent, it is very important that employees understand and support the values of the company and have belief in them.

The following chart will give an overview of factors that influence your employees' brand commitment.

Through these four key influencers, strong commitment can be achieved if:

- The company's mission and vision is communicated throughout the team and everybody knows what is expected of them.
- The mission of the company makes them feel like their work is important.
- On a regular basis, they receive recognition or praise for doing good work.
- Their supervisor, or someone at work, seems to care about them as a person and encourages their development.
- They have opportunities to learn and grow.

STAGES OF EMPLOYEE COMMITMENT

Internal branding is all about aligning employee commitment to the delivery of the brand promise of your organisation. To understand how the actions of your employees influence the image of your brand, let's take a look at the different levels of commitment your employees can manifest.

A: Total Connection

These employees have a desire to work to the point of exceeding expectations. They are driven to succeed and have set their own personal goals to climb the corporate ladder. They will ensure that the brand is communicated at all touch points.

B: Active Compliance

These employees have a willingness to do what is required – no more, no less. You can rely on these people to deliver your brand promise as directed, but don't expect them to come up with their own suggestions for improvements at ground level. With these employees, as long as you have your systems in place to deliver the brand promise at all touch points, they will be delivered accordingly at all touch points manned by these employees.

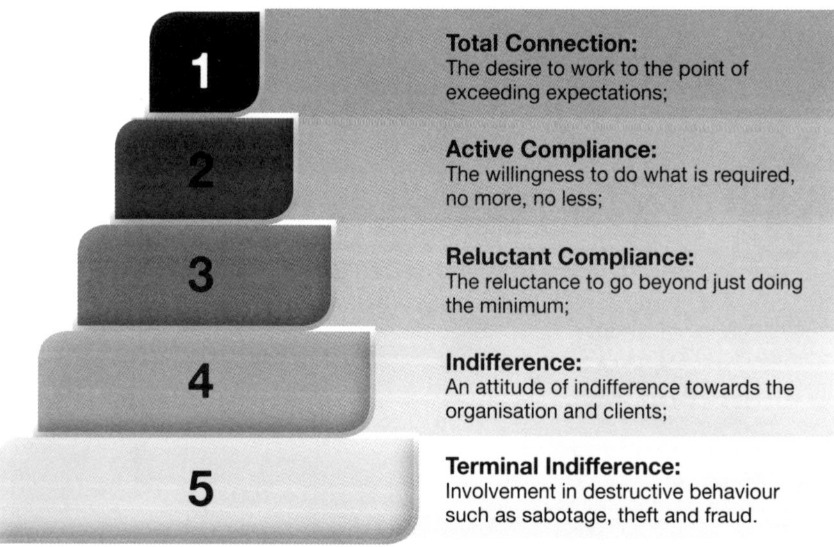

1
Total Connection:
The desire to work to the point of exceeding expectations;
2
Active Compliance:
The willingness to do what is required, no more, no less;
3
Reluctant Compliance:
The reluctance to go beyond just doing the minimum;
4
Indifference:
An attitude of indifference towards the organisation and clients;
5
Terminal Indifference:
Involvement in destructive behaviour such as sabotage, theft and fraud.

Longitudinal research conducted across multiple industries by IziCwe Academy

C: Reluctant Compliance
These employees are reluctant to go beyond just doing the minimum. They are not inspired to deliver your brand. It is enough for them to turn up for work and do enough to remain employed. They do not see the bigger picture, but only how they fit into the immediate workplace. Additional training will be a chore and it is unlikely that they will change their daily practices with additional training.

D: Indifference
These employees are simply filling time at your expense. They will have no ambition to rise higher within the company ranks, and are completely indifferent to the success or failure of the company. They will accept no responsibility for how their actions may affect your brand promise and won't care whether the customer's experience is a good one. If left unsupervised, they are unlikely to make any contribution at all, let alone do the job they were employed to do.

E: Terminal Indifference
The behaviour of these employees is destructive to your organisation. They will be involved in sabotage, theft or fraud, putting your organisation at harm.

Understanding the types of employees you have at your disposal will help in future recruitment drives. Obviously, you will be looking for types A & B as these are the ones that are capable of delivering an excellent brand experience for your customers and will respond well to training courses that will facilitate that brand delivery.

Research at over 1,500 corporate companies representing more than four million employees has shown employee commitment to average at 3.4 – between reluctant compliance and indifference.

Hewitt Associates Employee Engagement Database

HOW TO STRENGTHEN COMMITMENT

- Share as much information and business data as you can and be honest about what the data means. Don't hide negative business development, since employees want to learn about the business. Trust between employees and their supervisors has a huge impact and will strengthen commitment.

- Make sure everybody gets the right information. Misinterpretation and a lack of clarity will cause confusion and can lead an employee to come to a wrong conclusion, especially in today's fast changing business environment. It's better to have checked too much than too little.

- Explain why changes are made at the company. When employees know why the company is implementing something, it is easier for them to get on board and support the initiative.

- Give an answer to the "What's in it for me" question to your employees. Regularly explaining how business processes and goals benefit not only the customers and the company but also the employee, will help strengthen his or her commitment.

- Get to know your colleagues, spend time together outside the office building and have some fun as a team, while discovering common interests. Employees who enjoy both the work and the people they work with are more willing to put in extra effort to help the team to achieve its goals.

Case Study: Southwest Airlines

Something must be different at Southwest Airlines. Established in 1967 and headquartered in Dallas, Texas, at Southwest everybody seems to be smiling and happy. People at Southwest Airlines just look like a very big family, having a good time together. And at the same time Southwest Airlines has, by many measures, been one of the most successful airlines in the United States.

But what makes the company so successful? Why do Southwest Airlines' flight attendants always seem happier than those at other airlines?

The LUV Attitude

Have Fun

Enjoy Work

Don't Take Yourself too Seriously

Maintain Balance and Perspective

Be a Passionate Team Player

There must be a smart business plan, but there is something else that Southwest Airlines takes seriously:

"You put your employees first and if you take care of them, then they will take good care of you, then your customers will come back, and your shareholders will like that, so it's really a unity," said Herb Kelleher, the airline's co-founder and former chairman.

Even though this sounds simple, Southwest's success is largely due to the competitive advantage they have achieved through its human resource practices, most of which fall under the rubric of internal branding.

The company is known for its thorough selecting and training processes of employees as they form the company in the end. The main characteristic by which an employee is selected is not their work experience but their attitude towards their job. Southwest is looking for what they call the "fun-LUVing attitude." (LUV is the company's symbol on the New York Stock Exchange.) When finally admitted to the team and trained to do their specific job, the employee then gets motivated in the engagement of the overall mission of the company. Besides all the official training processes it is the overall family feeling they spread inside the company. Since its founding as "the LUV airline," Southwest has consistently nurtured its brand internally, to the point that it's now part of the company's DNA. The desire to meet excellent customer service, safety, and on-time performance drives the whole team at every level. Even when problems arise, they will work with motivation on solving the issue and realign towards the primary goals. It is very beneficial that all employees know how their jobs contribute to Southwest Airlines overall goals.

KEY INSIGHT

Key Insights of Chapter 5

- Commitment towards the brand is closely related to the concept of an individual's loyalty to the brand.
- Commitment to the company and its brand is initiated by internal support and communication, rewards and recognition, as well as personal and organisational values.
- An employee will have more commitment if a supervisor cares about and encourages the person's development.
- Differentiate the types of employee commitment and stay with the people with active compliance and total commitment. Others might work better in a different position.
- Check out the opportunities you have to strengthen commitment and get everybody on board.
- Commitment begins in the boardroom and the executive suite. If the top managers are not dedicated to the long-term success of the brand, those working underneath them won't be either.

Chapter 6:

3C - CONNECTION

During our 2012-2013 Internal Brand Engagement Survey we also learnt that only 17% of employees were truly connected to their brand. Forty percent were not connected, and the rest were only somewhat connected.

In most companies, the 17% who are connected will bring in disproportionally more revenue than the others. But these 17% who are connected can't carry the company. The other 83% who are somewhat connected or not connected need to be brought into alignment with the company's internal brand, and must be made to understand the importance of their connection to the products and services, and to the concept of meeting or exceeding customer expectations.

WHAT DOES CONNECTION MEAN?

Having a connection as an employee to the brand means having belief in the brand, a relationship to the organisation's identity, to the people they work with, and to their day-to-day work. Having such an aspirational, emotional and also intellectual connection with the brand leads to loyalty among the employee. This will improve the overall work experience, be delivered to and appreciated by the customer, and may result in increased revenues.

The Pareto Effect of Brand Connection

But unfortunately, very often employee performance follows the Pareto Principle, the 80/20 rule which means that anything a few do is vital but what the bulk does is trivial. In the case of employee connection, a high proportion of employees are weak and disinterested performers who do just enough not to get fired, and the smaller proportion of employees are passionate and engaged performers making the difference.

This smaller percentage represents those employees who are intellectually and emotionally connected, and their interests, talents and skills are matched to their work. These employees perform at significantly greater levels than the lackadaisical and unhappy employees. The reason for the increased performance is the emotional connection the employees feel to their jobs. Employees who become emotionally connected to their work will perform better.

EMPLOYEE BELIEF

Your employees need to feel emotionally connected with your brand. Once you have established the belief systems, you need to get your people connected to the business. They must believe in the:

- **Aspirational**

They must believe in the big picture. When an employee just focuses on his individual role, the customer tends to receive the "it's not my job" kind of service. The employee needs to understand that the ultimate goal of the business is to deliver the brand promise and not to define who can or cannot deliver it. It becomes the employee's role to aspire to deliver outside of their immediate job role.

> ***Example:***
> *If a customer has language barriers with the taxi driver who has just brought the person to the hotel, any bilingual person from the hotel staff – a maid or waiter – could help out if nobody else was available.*

- **Inspirational**

They must believe in the authenticity of the brand. The employee must be able to sell the idea of the brand convincingly.

If you run a delicatessen, you need staff who love the food and are able to enthusiastically recommend choice cuts of meat to your customers. A vegetarian or animal rights activist is unlikely to suit the position!

> ***Example:***
> *If you go to The Body Shop, their employees are all convinced of The Body Shop's values and mission to protect the planet, defend human rights, support community trade, and ensure everything is animal cruelty free. It's not just part of their jobs, it's part of their personal conviction. That makes the customer experience credible.*

- **Emotional**

They must feel a sense of ownership. Internal branding will help to build an emotional connection for the employee with the brand in the same way that external branding builds the same kind of connection for the customer. The employee will become an ambassador for the brand in the same way that the customer becomes an advocator for the brand.

Example:
A very strong emotional connection can result from a personal experience. For example, if a woman successfully lost weight using a dieting product, she will have a very strong connection to the brand when working for the company that is producing the product or working as a sales person.

- **Functional**

They must believe in the products and services you offer. It is hard to sell a product or service that you don't believe in. An essential part of employment with your company is that the employee supports and believes in the products and services they deliver. If your employee is not athletic and watches TV all day, he or she is unlikely to be able to effectively sell gym memberships or sporting goods.

Example:
Imagine any Apple store around the world, where staff is promoting and selling those coveted iPhones, iPads and MacBooks. How would you react if he told you about the great apps and features the new IPhone offered while you heard the typical Samsung sound coming out of his pocket?

RE-CONNECTING EMPLOYEES WITH THE BRAND

Now, let's focus on the other side. How can you tell somebody isn't building a connection and how can that be changed for the better? If you have noticed some of the following points at your workplace, your employees or colleagues are probably not having a strong connection to the company's brand.

- Employees show no passion for the brand
- Employees are bored at work
- Employees are constantly having a negative attitude towards their employer brand or colleagues
- High rate of absenteeism
- Customer complaints about poor service
- Infighting among employees

Sometimes it takes only some little things to re-connect someone with the brand, resulting in a huge impact not only on the person but on the whole team.

Reconnect employees

Try to customise the job more around your employee's talents and interests but in a way that is still meaningful to the business. Use a talent assessment to identify natural strengths. Employees who are very social and talkative are better in service, sales or other roles that put them in front of customers. Or for supportive, engaging people the work should be arranged as teamwork as often as possible. Aligning employees to roles that use their natural abilities makes them feel more connected and engaged. Here are some more ideas how small changes can re-connect an employee:

- An employee from the sales department who is also a talented writer may improve his or her connection to the job if they can also prepare the company's newsletter or write a monthly column for the intranet.
- A finance employee who is also a good organiser may feel more emotionally connected to the company if he or she is involved in organising a company's teambuilding event, meeting, or product launch.
- A senior manager who has been working with the company for many years may feel honoured to share some personal stories and talk about his connection to younger employees. This can guide the new hires in their performance and strengthen cohesion.

The Case for Employee Loyalty

If your internal brand is able to consistently connect with its employees on an emotional level, it is much more likely to achieve strong employee loyalty. Consider some recent studies: MetLife's 10th annual survey of employee benefits, trends and attitudes released in March puts employee loyalty at a seven-year low. One in three employees, the survey says, plans to leave his or her job by the end of the year. According to a 2011 Careerbuilder.com report, 76% of full-time workers would leave their current workplace if the right opportunity came along. Other studies show that each year, on the average a company loses anywhere from 20% to 50% of its employee base.

The key is that emotional connection that can be built between the employee and their brand that engages them and gives them that belief and connection to the brand.

Case Study: Banyan Tree Hotel & Resort

snapshot from www.banyantree.com

This Singapore-based company has grown from its flagship operation in Thailand into a global brand in part by focusing considerable effort on aligning its employees to the brand. By establishing a strong workforce, Banyan Tree has shown consistently low turnover with a high level of commitment of the staff. This has been accomplished through the utilisation of resources and the offer of generous benefits and rewards. Since then, more than half of the staff have taken up these benefits and have given good feedback.

For example, a complimentary hotel stay on a Banyan Tree property (worth US$2,000 to US$5,000) is given to each employee every year. This reward is to bond the family and can be accumulated over two years so that the employee and his or her family can enjoy an extended vacation.

Another one is the Honeymoon Benefit, which applies when a Banyan Tree employee gets married. The person will receive a complimentary three-night stay at any of the company's hotels. In addition, the couple is given a cash gift of US$500.

To Claire Chiang, the senior vice president, the "why" behind this is pretty clear: "A winning organisation addresses the work-life needs of its employees, and in doing so, realises the benefit of efficiency and productivity via an empowered and enabled workforce."

It's no wonder that Banyan Tree won the Work-Life Achiever Award 2008 and it is no wonder they have such a connected workforce to the brand.

KEY INSIGHT

Key Insights of Chapter 6

- Having a connection as an employee to the brand means having belief in the brand.
- Your employees must believe in "the big picture" and have a connection to the brand, the product, and the company.
- The connection builds on the aspirational, inspirational, emotional, and functional believe in the brand
- Following the Pareto principle, a high proportion of employees are often weak and disinterested performers who do just enough not to get fired, and only the smaller proportion of employees are passionate and engaged performers. You can change that!

Chapter 7:

4C - CONSISTENCY

In our survey, only 57% of employees stated that they reflect their brand consistently across their key touchpoints. Critically, 43% did not reflect their brand all day, every day.

The implications are serious. An effective internal branding scheme must be applied consistently and over time. Too many companies make a big "splash" with an internal branding programme, only to let it wither. This produces the feeling of inconsistency and leads employees to believe that the company is only interested in short-term, easy goals.

Companies like Infosys, Cathay Pacific, McDonald's, and IBM have earned their customers' trust through consistently delivering the brand promise over years. Like these examples show, the strongest brands in the world have been around for a long time and they intend to be here for a long time to come. To become such a strong, long time market player it is important to make strategic decisions accordingly. Brand value builds over time through consistently living the brand promise. This consistency is essential for a brand as it helps to deliver trust and confidence for the customer as well as clarity of positioning and purpose and is therefore directly linked to reliability. A consistent brand has an identity for itself, a soul that should not change even though it must continually adapt to the ever-changing business environment. Consistent, brand-oriented employee behaviour is a critical success factor in achieving this.

Each time your business interacts with a customer or the public, the touch points are the moments of truth for your brand promise. At every point of contact with your customer, you must convey your brand experience and carry this through. Touch points convey internal processes to external customers. Inconsistency at touch points will leave customers feeling the difference and experiencing a lack of integration. Every point of contact with your customer should consistently convey your brand,

- Be it over telephone, through direct mail, on your website, or through your processes,
- Through profiles on Facebook, Twitter, and YouTube,
- Either indirectly or face to face,
- From January through December,
- 24/7,
- From security staff to senior managers.

There should never be a question whether the customer has interacted with a different company that just happens to bear the same name. Ensure that each employee is empowered to identify and address inconsistencies in your brand.

Activity Template:

State some of your Key Touchpoints and state the role your brand values/vision/mission play in impacting these touchpoints:

State Touchpoint	Touchpoint 1	Touchpoint 2	Touchpoint 3
Brand Vision			
Brand Mission			
Brand Value 1			

Case Study: McDonald's

With over 33,000 locations worldwide that serve about 68 million customers every day, McDonald's is one of the most well known brands on earth. Considering the size of McDonald's, it is easy to imagine how one could lose control with both the internal and the external branding effort. Just a few years ago, this caused McDonald's to face a huge challenge regarding their brand image. The company faced aggressive competition, a decreasing share price, and many negative customer experience reports.

To improve performance McDonald's recognised that it needed to make a plan with clear objectives: The first was to improve overall management practices to align employees to the business strategy, and the second to ensure that every employee was held accountable for improving performance. The senior management in partnership with the global HR group passed an improvement plan, which included a variety of management practices designed to strengthen alignment among all employees. To change employees' attitude towards the brand and to create a high-performance culture, McDonald's analysed its current performance practices and designed an integrated approach to support the organisation.

As McDonald's founder Ray Kroc had once emphasised "We are not in the hamburger business, we are in the people business." With this in mind, McDonald's refocused on aligning its employees to the company.

After all, the plan did not only provide a structure to align individual performance goals with business strategies, but also fostered individual growth. It further supported individual performance evaluation based on results achieved, and then identified, developed and rewarded positive development. The two-year foundation degree in managing business operations offered at McDonald's University is one demonstration of how seriously the company takes the training of its staff.

Within this, the main part of the internal branding at McDonald's occurs through their extensive training and development programme, which all employees have to follow. All employees working at McDonald's have to go through a standardised programme of training; the company's goal is to become the best talent developer with employees committed to the McDonald's brand mantra, "Quality, Service, Cleanliness & Value."

After these establishments and changes were made the company delivered stronger business results and received improved customer feedback. Ensuring alignment of individual performance goals with the brand strategy, was a critical enabler to McDonald's brand success.

KEY INSIGHT

Key Insights of Chapter 7

- Strong brands develop over a long period of time through consistently delivering on the brand promise.
- Every touch point needs to support the brand promise.
- If employees deliver a customer experience on an inconsistent basis, the customer will feel a lack of integration.
- As McDonald's proved, it is never too late to focus on the brand consistency and deliver your promises.

Chapter 8:

5C - CHAMPIONING

Our survey results indicated that 60% of employees said that their leaders walk the talk, but only 40% claim that they themselves mentor and help create other brand champions.

What does this mean? It means that too many frontline employees are not sufficiently invested in the success of the company to take the long-range view and mentor employees who are beneath them. Mentoring is not immediately rewarding; it is a process that takes time. The company must make it clear that it is not interested only in this quarter's profits, but supports long-term efforts devoted to growth and the brand promise.

Every corporate brand needs, their brand champions, who promote and refer your business to others. Brand champions are passionate about the brand. You need these champions within your company.

Have you ever met someone who swears they will only ever buy a Toyota car? That person is a brand champion. The person who goes to the supermarket and buys only Colgate toothpaste? Also a brand champion. Or the man who is loyal to an English premier league football team even though he has never even been to England before? A brand champion.

While brand champions can be any stakeholder, we're going to focus on your employees as brand champions. Every brand champion impacts and conveys the brand to various target groups and determines the brand's success or failure. While today's new products and services can become tomorrow's commodities, the one thing your competitors cannot copy is your employees' relationship with your customers.

A brand champion:

- Defends passionately his or her brand as the right choice.
- Actively talks to others about their brand experience.
- Influences sales through their word of mouth support.
- Becomes an expert on a brand and product.

Whether your goals are to build your business brand or your personal brand, you have to fill the role of brand champions. If you and your employees can't demonstrate how much you believe in your brand, why should anyone else believe in it?

HOW TO STRENGTHEN YOUR BRAND CHAMPIONS

Employees:

- Develop brand training that exposes each employee to the brand's core values and capabilities.
- Give them "material" to tell about the experience with your brand and explain the brand promise or key positioning. This could include the company's proud history.
- Empower them to create stories and lead conversations about your brand to influence others.
- Reward their enthusiasm for your brand.
- Provide employees with apparel with the brand logo and tagline.
- Offer educational opportunities that can help employees improve your product offering or service.
- Let them participate in brand development, e.g. internally passing on branding-relevant customer feedback from customer touch points.

Management:

- Be sure that executives understand and are loyal to the brand values.
- Provide management with apparel with the brand logo and mission statement.
- With every decision made that affects the brand, be sure that the information flows down efficiently to everybody else.
- Make them go through a mentorship training programme, so that they are empowered to do the same for their team members.

At the end of the day, brand champions will deliver a winning game plan. Branding is a team sport in the strictest sense of the word. If you have a tendency to do it individually, you have a high chance of failure. Your best chance at winning is when you allow employees to become part of the branding team. Together you can fight and surpass the competition!

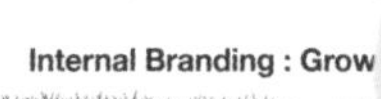

CASE STUDY

Case Study: Famous brand champions

Instead of looking at one specific company, the following examples will give you insight into brand champions you probably already know. Many of the biggest brands we all know have a person who continually advocates the brand, is the living embodiment of the brand promise, and protects the brand from negative publicity. What comes to your mind when you hear the names of Bill Gates, Steve Jobs, or even Gandhi? You automatically think of the brands they have championed and an immediate perception of the brand comes to mind.

The Facebook brand champion: Mark Zuckerberg

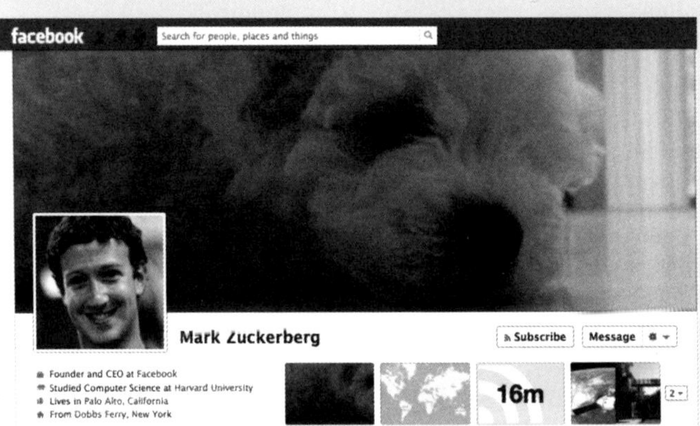

Mark Zuckerberg, who started his business from his college dormitory room, became the youngest self-made billionaire in history by creating a new method of communication for individuals around the world. While initially launched as a social medium to connect with his friends at Harvard, Facebook quickly grew and soon counted millions of members, including individuals and organisations, and was available in more than 70 languages. Mark Zuckerberg is the name behind this huge empire, giving the brand a face – a champion - and people make that association. In 2012, Zuckerberg went to a presentation with investors wearing a casual hoodie, which caused Wall Street financial analysts to publicly accuse Zuckerberg of immaturity. By not wearing a suit and tie to such an important event, they alleged, Zuckerberg was telling potential shareholders they wouldn't matter. But many voices across the nation rushed to his defence, explaining that the hoodie was a symbol of his independent-mindedness, his authenticity, and brand personality. We will sure be hearing much more from this brand champion in the future.

The Apple brand champion: Steve Jobs

Apple and Steve Jobs exemplified a relationship between a brand and a person. He perfectly represented the vision, mission and promise of the Apple brand. Through his inspiring leadership he made Apple one of the most successful brands in the world. While holding the chief executive position of Apple as well as guardian and ambassador of the brand, it allowed Jobs to take a very holistic approach to the brand at a very strategic level. He demanded big results and became the strongest brand champion as a brand innovator. Now that he has passed, his spirit will be serving as the champion for the Apple brand for a long time.

The Microsoft brand champion: Bill Gates

Bill Gates is one of the richest men in the world, not only because he is a smart guy, entrepreneur, and chairman of the Microsoft Corporation, but also because of his devotion and loyalty to his brand. The Microsoft brand and also its co-founder Bill Gates are known globally and need no introduction. The brand was built on the vision of Gates and his collaborators including Steve Ballmer and Paul Allen, who embarked on their journey when Gates was a student at Harvard. In 1976, only a few months before graduation, Harvard informed Gates that it was against university policy to allow a student to run a business in a dormitory. Rather than abandon Microsoft, Gates chose to drop out. It goes to show you that being a Brand Champion is something that is innate in all of us, regardless of where we came from and our challenges.

KEY INSIGHT

Key Insights of Chapter 8

- Brand champions promote and refer your business to others.
- They actively talk to others about the brand experience.
- They encourage their peers and colleagues to embrace and project the brand with their passion.
- Every employee can be a brand champion!
- Branding is a team sport and with brand champions you will win the game.

PART 3:
HOW?

Chapter 9:

MAKING IT ALL HAPPEN

THE INTERNAL BRAND STRATEGY ACTION PLAN

In the rest of this book, we will explore the 6-Step Internal Brand Strategy Action Plan – a plan that will help you establish your Internal Brand and help you connect with your employees.

> Virgin is one company that has always recognised the importance of its people. Its attitude is demonstrated in its new group brand manual: "Chapter One -- Our People Come First." "We have always believed that to create a powerful external brand you need to create a culture that supports it," adds Catherine Salway, Group Brand Manager for Virgin.
> Yet the process of creating and maintaining a brand culture in the workplace -- internal brand alignment -- is a difficult and delicate one. It needs more than a manual and a slide presentation. Alignment is about encouraging employees to behave in certain ways. And that means ensuring that you have a process in place that can impact the hearts and minds of your employees. It is not just about imposing a brand culture but really about knowing your brand and creating a model for change that you know will resonate with your employees and for your brand.

SETTING UP THE INTERNAL BRAND TASK FORCE TEAM A.K.A. BRAND CHAMPIONS

Getting the support of your employees is a critical start. One of the things to do is to create a task force compromising of key members across branding, communication, marketing, human resource and senior leadership. The key purpose of the task force will be to:

1. Establish the goals

First establish logical connections such as the goals of the initiative. These can be qualitative or quantitative. Powerful goals include increasing awareness, building new attitudes and behaviour change. Goals could also be increasing employee loyalty or customer satisfaction.

2. Set individual roles

Each member of your team should be on the same page and take on tasks and responsibilities. Use your strengths in the roles. For example members of the team that work in HR might handle the training components, while those in marketing and corporate communication could handle research and communication.

3. Guide with strategies

One of the biggest problems we face when we consult companies is that decisions are sometimes based on gut feel. I have met a few leaders who ignore all research and go with what they think is right. While there is nothing wrong in doing that and there have been some success stories, it is more the exception than the rule. Quality research can help your brand become more relevant and provide you with ammunition for your strategies. Take a step back from your brand and let yourself be guided by the research which in turn will guide your strategy.

4. Take action

Setting strategies alone is not enough if you don't put them into action. Ensure that once the strategy is in place, the task force works towards getting it executed across critical touchpoints.

5. Measure progress

Throughout the process ensure that the task force is always tracking results and ensuring that goals are met.

Once you have the team in place with the right mindset, the strategy to building your Internal brand begins. One of the things that we tell our clients is that communicating the brand values to staff requires the same methods as external brand marketing campaign. You need to segment your internal population just as you would your external audience and communicate appropriately. Communication needs to be relevant, and in today's climate, experiential as well. This could be through rallies, workshops, online training, even picnics but everything should be driven by your brand strategy.

Take a look at the following **Chain of Brand Performance** chart to see the impact on your business once your internal and external brand start to work in synchronisation.

Establishing a clear brand strategy with your employees will ensure that your brand is communicated externally. More than that, it will produce a happy and productive workforce that will drive your brand promise to your customers. This will lead to improved service and products, value attraction in the market, and ultimately brand loyalty and customer retention. The financial impact of the alignment of your internal and external brand can result in a stronger market position, higher revenues, increased brand value, a higher ROI, a higher share price, and increased M&A position.

For now, let us introduce the Action Plan, which we will explore in the following chapters. Follow these steps in order and your organisation can end up with a strong internal brand positioning that will align your employees with your brand promise and establish brand loyalty with your customers.

INTERNAL BRAND STRATEGY ACTION PLAN

The Internal Brand Strategy Action Plan is in six logical stages as follows:

1 Brand Research *(Ch. 10)*

In this initial step, we will look at auditing our present internal brand so that we can set our goals and objectives. We will conduct research so that we can base our actions on established facts.

2 Strategic Blueprint - Brand DNA *(Ch. 11)*

The second stage will involve understanding, creating or refining our brand platform. This is essentially proposing the heart of our plan of action and communicating this across our organisation.

3 Motivation and Internal Training *(Ch. 12)*

The goal for training is to create our brand ambassadors, setting up systems to ensure that our employees are living the brand, and creating strategies that will motivate our employees.

4 Communicate: Delivering the Experience *(Ch. 13)*

Communicating the brand is important in ensuring that the internal brand is communicated effectively to employees. Having a strategic internal communication plan that allows us to build awareness and change mindsets, which is important at this stage.

5 Support Systems *(Ch. 14)*

Ensuring that our internal brand is driven across our organisation is critical. It should be seen in everything we do including how we recognise, reward and review staff performance.

6 Brand Performance Measurement *(Ch. 15)*

This is a crucial final stage in setting our internal branding into motion. It is not enough to have the internal brand be effective in the short term and then be left to run on itself. Like any machine, this too will need oiling and regular maintenance to work. We will need to review our internal branding strategies on a regular basis, and to do this we need to accurately and consistently measure our brand performance. This stage will take us through the measurement programme, introduce the Brand Scorecard, and review our marketing ROI.

Each of the following chapters will introduce you to the six steps of the Brand Theatre Action Plan one after another.

Case Study: Yahoo!

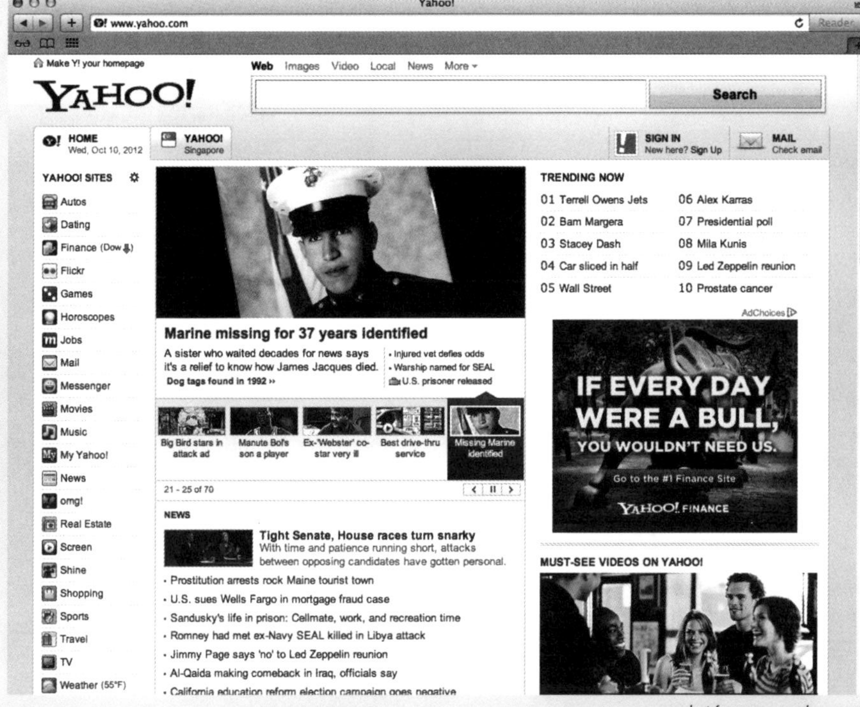

snapshot from www.yahoo.com

In 2001, Libby Sartain started her job as chief people officer at Yahoo! Inc. She entered a demoralised company without a well-defined culture. During her first year at Yahoo! the company became a victim of the dot-com bubble and for the first time Yahoo! was forced to lay off a substantial part of its employees, including senior executives. Predictably, morale at Yahoo! was shaken. The company, founded in 1994 in Sunnyvale, California, saw its post-bubble stock price hit a low of US$4.05 on September 26, 2001, only eighteen months after reaching a high of US$118.75 a share on January 3, 2000.

It took several years, but the organisation overcame some crucial challenges. As part of its rebuilding efforts, Yahoo! launched a comprehensive internal branding campaign to transform the company's start-up culture into one that was built for the long term. This internal branding initiative was designed to position the company for a profitable future.

The branding process began with research, an employee survey, and a series of meetings with founders, employees, and executives. It was clear that Yahoo! had to define its mission and values. But to some of the people in charge, corporate values seemed too traditional for such an impulsive young company. One of the founders asked, "Why do we have to have a list of values? Why can't we just have a list of 'what sucks?' " And yes, this is exactly how they marketed the values, paired with a "What-sucks-and-aren't-you-glad-you-won't-find-these-at-Yahoo!" list.

These values and anti-values became the foundation for the new Yahoo! brand. As they launched the rebranding, the marketing and HR department also conducted an internal review of the company. Workshops were held to explore brand characteristics, competencies, values, and territories. A brand audit was conducted with internal stakeholders through one-on-one interviews.

After finishing the research Yahoo! kept improving its internal brand positioning and applying it to every dimension of the employee experience with the overall goal to keep Yahoos with the "Y! gene." A coordinated method to communicate with employees was introduced and processes, policies, and procedures developed. In the end, the way employees design, deliver, and communicate the brand had changed.

The Yahoo! "Life Engine" with everything a customer needs or wants to do was then also introduced internally. Efforts were made to align employees around the brand. This involved finding the unique attributes that attract the right people and that created the right experience for Yahoo! employees, allowing them to bring out their best. For example, they held an essay contest for employees and customers to describe how Yahoo! was their Life Engine, with a Harley-Davidson as the prize.

Due to this alignment of the employee experience with the customer experience and the brand promise, a powerful relationship with employees was established.

KEY INSIGHT

Key Insights of Chapter 9

- The Chain of Brand Performance chart shows the impact your internal and external branding can have when they work in synchronization.
- Create a team of Brand Champions to drive your Internal Brand initiatives.
- First you need a clear brand strategy. Then you need to develop a productive workforce that will drive your brand promise to your customers. Finally, your brand needs to be well communicated externally.
- This will lead to improved service and products, value attraction in the market, and ultimately brand loyalty and customer retention.

Chapter 10:

STEP 1 - BRAND RESEARCH

1 Brand Research

2 Strategic Blueprint - Brand DNA

3 Motivation and Internal Training

4 Communicate: Delivering the Experience

5 Support Systems

6 Brand Performance Measurement

RESEARCH THE EFFECT OF YOUR BRANDING

Targeted research, carried out to establish how effectively your internal and external brand is communicated, is an invaluable exercise that will correct any common or assumed misconceptions and allow you to address areas that need your attention. The results of the research will help to assess past brand performance and give you a roadmap for improvements.

The Role of Brand Audits

Brand audits provide qualitative brand snapshots that allow you to benchmark your current brand position by revealing how your brand is perceived both internally and by the customer. You will be able to assess strengths and weaknesses in your service, marketing, and quality of products.

But brand audits do much more than that. They can also unify your organisation. Without a strong internal brand messaging and communication, you essentially leave the interpretation of your brand up to your employees. In this situation, it is likely that your employees will develop a different definition of what your brand stands for. A brand audit can illustrate these differences in perception and provide you with a roadmap for building a consistent, organisation-wide accepted vision of the brand. This is crucial to ensure that everyone is on the same page.

Finally, brand audits can help align your company's belief in its brand with that of your customers.

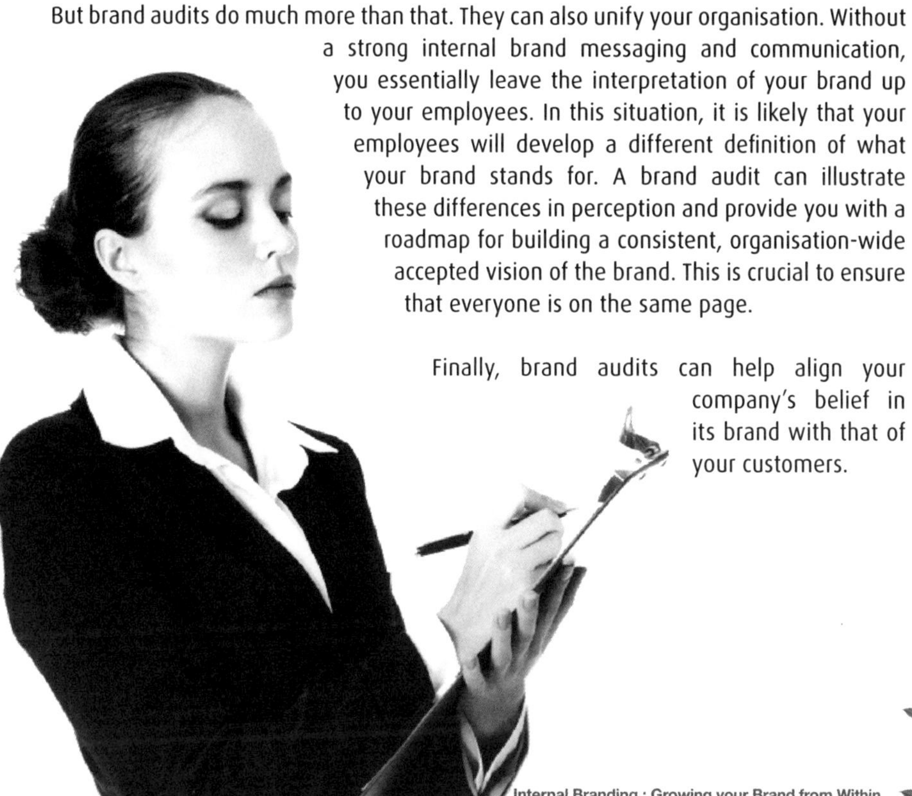

INTERNAL BRAND AUDIT

An internal brand audit involves an in-depth assessment of the attitudes and beliefs of your individual employees from corporate executive level downwards. One-on-one confidential interviews are designed to assess each manager's perceptions of the brand, the company's branding goals, evaluation of past branding activities, and knowledge of key brand messages.

In your one-on-one interviews, you can consider putting the following to your management staff:

- **What is our core brand value?**
- **Where are your employees at currently in terms of loyalty/ motivation/ alignment?**
- **Describe a typical customer/employee and his or her expectations and requirements.**
- **What past internal marketing activity has been the most successful in terms of promoting brand? What past marketing activity has been least successful?**
- **What experience would you offer the customer and your employee?**

The responses to the interviews are then carefully analysed and presented. Often our clients are surprised at how much corporate brand visions and values vary between departments, branches and individuals. If your company as a whole can't get its message straight, how is the customer supposed to be able to understand your brand?

An internal brand audit does more than simply assess attitudes and beliefs. It is an important tool in testing the quality of service and responsiveness.

The Mystery Shopper Audit

A Mystery shopper programme is when we hire customers to engage with customer facing staff and report to us on their experience. With a mystery shopper programme, you can anonymously experience the company from the customer's viewpoint at all employee facing customer touch points. The resulting report will reveal the level of responsiveness and the quality of the interaction. Again, results can be surprising. You may find problems with the attitudes or performances of your employees, inadequate information conveyed, and poor service as a result of complacency or lack of training.

Most of your customers will not bother to complain about such shortcomings, and nothing will change to improve them unless you conduct a Mystery Shopper Audit.

INTERNAL COMMUNICATIONS AUDIT

A communications audit is more appropriate for larger organisations with multiple departments and branches. A communications audit looks at all the material that communicates the brand to the employees including brochures, websites, events and speeches. The audit will compare each for consistency of brand messaging, visual style, and adherence to corporate guidelines and brand strategy. From this, you can create a brand manual to ensure that the brand values are followed throughout the organisation.

Things to consider for your brand guidelines are:

- Your key messages - Are these consistent across all channels and media?
- Are corporate standards followed?
- Is there a common look and feel that communicates your brand?
- How current is information?
- Are your brand vision and values accurately portrayed?

You should conduct your internal communications audit at the same time as an internal brand audit.

The Brand Within™ Tool

We talked a bit about generic research tools, so it is perhaps important that we share our Internal Audit research tool which we call Brand Within™. This tool measures the loyalty between employees and the brand, and aims to provide data that can help understand the motivation and value of the brand with that of the beliefs and behaviours of the employees.

Remember our 5Cs from the earlier chapters? This model consists of 5 critical areas based on the Cs. Namely, understanding of the brand by the employees, the connection and belief the employees have with the brand, their commitment and alignment to the brand. The tool also measures the impact of internal communications as well as employee loyalty to the brand.

Typically when we run this tool we look at gaps and opportunities. We look at creating a strategy, amending strategy or assessing areas of weakness through this tool.

CLARITY	COMMITMENT	CONNECTION	CONSISTENCY	CHAMPION
Importance of having a clear business vision Knowledge of brand	Employee loyalty & commitment Employee pride Employee advocacy Identification of areas of opportunities	Performance across key brand values Importance of each brand value Recommen-dations for internal brand strategy	Alignment of internal behaviors Impact of internal communications Recommendations for brand alignment	Understanding of work contributions to corporate goals Do our leaders walk the talk Recommendations for internal mentoring Recommendations for internal communications

Internal Brand Research Exercise

CLARITY	COMMITMENT	CONNECTION	CONSISTENCY	CHAMPION
Do our Staff know our brand? Do they understand it?	How committed are they to our brand? How loyal are our employees?	Are our Staff connected to our brand? Do they believe in the big picture of our brand?	Do they apply the brand consistently in everything they do? How consistent are our internal communica-tions and key touchpoints? What is the best communication strategy to use to reach to our staff?	Will they go the extra mile to deliver the brand promise? Do our leaders walk the talk and how can we impact our employees to think like Brand Champions?

In the essence, research is done to give answers to these questions: What are the gaps in my brand?

Current Condition What have I learnt?	**Gap Analysis**	**Ideal Condition** Where do I want to be?
External Perspective How does my customer see my brand?	List down all the gaps between your current condition in this space	**External Perspective** I want my customer to associate my brand with:
Internal Perspective How does my employee see my brand?		**External Perspective** I want my employee to associate my brand with:

CASE STUDY

Case Study: The Casino Merger

When the seventh largest US casino operator purchased another casino, the total size of the organisation was doubled. To make the merger an overall success, the management wanted to integrate an identifiable, corporate service culture.

The overall objective for all properties was to spark a distinct culture and a branded experience that would be delivered consistently throughout all properties. This involved tackling two major challenges: To reduce the high staff turnover and to ensure the management style of both organisations is aligned with their new brand elements. The target also was to ensure the effective delivery of the personal side of customer service as a key business strategy by teaching personal customer service skills and attitudes that would inspire all frontline employees to implement specifically defined customer service skills and behaviours. It further meant to inspire the support from the management team throughout all levels of the organisation.

The process started with the project team members conducting site visits at each property, identifying logistics, key players, and key needs, and also completing company wide anonymous culture audits. Staff members were selected as Brand Champions at each property. A wide management briefing was held to gain corporate buy-in for the brand implementation programme and a one-day management briefing for managers and supervisors held at each location to share culture audit findings. The brand promise was built around an existing acronym that the casino used. It became a part of the daily language of the casino.

Building in activities was critical for the success of a programmes of this type, and the training of the casino's internal facilitators has been a major success factor of this total project. In the meantime, the organisation has shifted into its second generation of leaders but the programmes is still being supported. In fact, it defines the casino's branded service.

The HR department continues to gather metrics across a wide range of the organisation's activities on a regular basis, including the efficacy of its training programmes. A mentoring programme has been established for new hires as well.

The casino brand has since won several awards for its internal operations, and staff turnover rates have been reduced from 60 percent to 34 percent, one of the lowest rates in the industry.

Article extracted from BRAND SNAP, Branded Customer Service, Janelle Barlow & Paul Stewart

KEY INSIGHT

Key Insights of Chapter 10

- Research will correct misconceptions and allow you to address areas that need your attention.
- Brand audits provide qualitative brand snapshots on how your brand is perceived both internally and by the external customer.
- An internal brand audit provides an in-depth view of the attitudes and beliefs of your individual employees from corporate executive level downwards.
- It will also inform you of the gap between the current internal brand condition with the ideal condition, thus helping you in understanding the key concerns.
- A communications audit looks at all the material that communicates the brand. The audit will compare each touchpont for consistency of brand messaging, visual style and adherence to corporate guidelines.

Chapter 11:

STEP 2 - STRATEGY BLUEPRINT- BRAND DNA

1 Brand Research

2 Strategic Blueprint - Brand DNA

3 Motivation and Internal Training

4 Communicate: Delivering the Experience

5 Support Systems

6 Brand Performance Measurement

In this chapter, we will look at how to create focus through your Brand DNA and your Brand Story.

Your Brand DNA will add spirit and soul to what would otherwise be a robotic, automated, generic price-value proposition. Later in this chapter, we will look at an example of how Starbucks have become the masters at adding spirit and soul into its brand.

> Southwest Airlines has built its culture and reputation by starting from the inside. Its leadership team defined the organisation's core values as well as its niche in the market, then maintained consistency as the airline grew, by ensuring all employees understand and embody the spirit of the organisation.
>
> FedEx has what it calls the "purple promise," a commitment to service excellence that is part of their employee culture. Every employee is called upon to work to fulfil that promise, even those whose jobs are not customer-facing. And it's not just an internal dialogue or initiative; the promise is part of their public website, with sections that highlight everyday activities by employees that fulfil that promise.

YOUR BRAND STRATEGY

Strong brands never happen by accident. Yet many companies do not take a disciplined approach to brand planning and execution.

> **While 80% of advertising and marketing professionals say they are strongly aware of their company's brand positioning, only one fourth of them "can clearly articulate their company's brand position to... clients, customers or prospective clients."**
>
> ***Louws Management Corporation Survey,*** *2007*

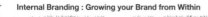

THE CUSTOMER - BRAND EMPLOYEE ENGAGEMENT DIAGRAM

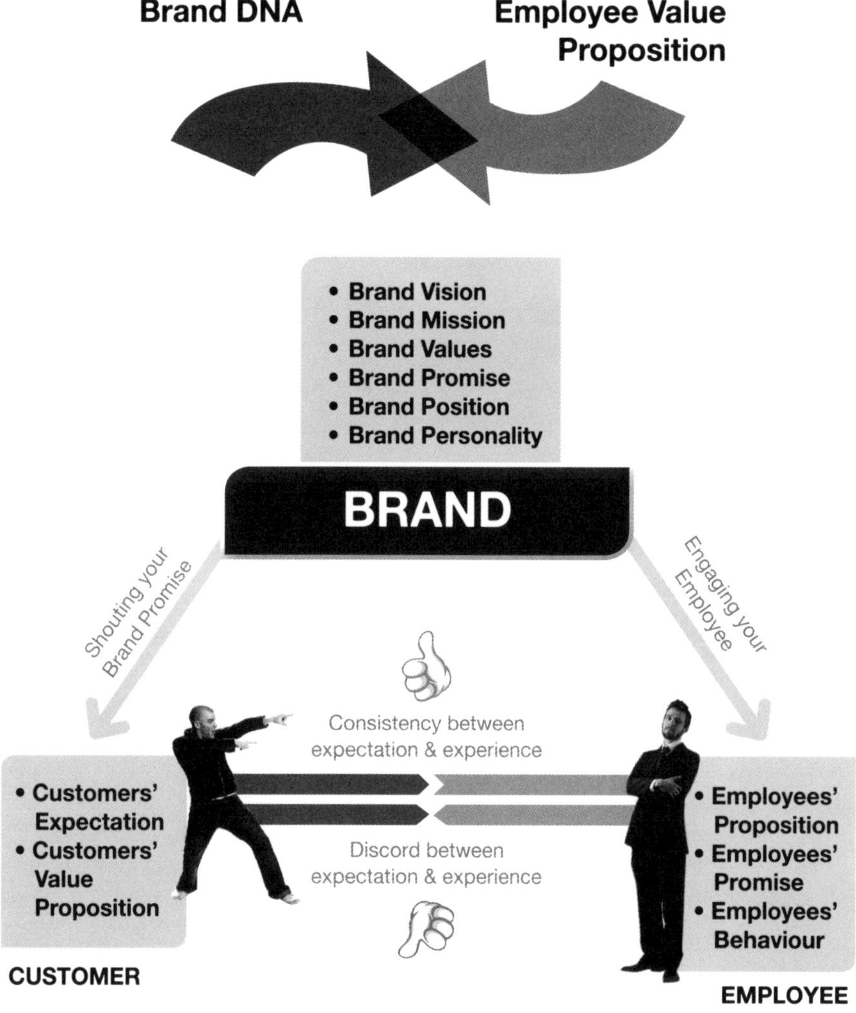

What your brand stands for

Your brand DNA is made up of six components:
1. **Brand vision:** What you are aiming for.
2. **Brand mission:** Why your brand exists.
3. **Brand promise:** The pledged experience.
4. **Brand values:** How the vision and promises are delivered.
5. **Brand position:** How you are seen in the market place.
6. **Brand personality:** What people associate with you and your brand story and identity.

It is the combination of all these attributes that makes up your brand vision that says what your brand stands for.

THE BRAND DNA COMPONENTS

We will look at each component of your brand DNA separately. To deliver your brand personality, your employees must understand your brand DNA in all its aspects so that they can confidently and unambiguously deliver your brand personality to your consumers.

1. Brand Vision

Your Vision is how you foresee where your company will be. Over time, as your company develops and achieves goals, your vision may change, so you will need to revisit your vision every five years or so.

Example

A few years ago, Pepsi's vision statement might as well have been simply, "Beat Coke." If you go onto their website today, you will find a values-based statement, adjusted to their current brand vision: "PepsiCo's responsibility is to continually improve all aspects of the world in which we operate - environment, social, economic - creating a better tomorrow than today."

2. Brand Mission

Your mission is the primary purpose of your company's existence - what you set out to do. It is the simple answer to the question "What does your company do?" Keep it as clear and succinct as possible so that when your employees meet their customers, in the first thirty seconds, they can communicate the mission statement to that prospect. If it is not clear for you, it won't be for the people you explain it to either. Don't be one of those people who talks to prospects for ten minutes, and after you have walked away they still don't know what you do!

Example

As you can find it on their website, the BMW Group's mission is to be "the world's leading provider of premium products and premium services for individual mobility".

3. Brand Promise

Your brand is a promise. This is the single most important thing you deliver to your customers. A brand's reputation and longevity depends on whether the company is able to consistently keep the brand promise. The employees play a crucial role in the success of your brand promise, for it is your employees that deliver it. If you have promised to deliver excellent service, it will only take one apathetic employee to ensure that you fail in delivering your brand promise. Your employees must know your promise, understand your promise, understand their role in delivering that promise, and have the necessary hard or soft skills required to deliver the promise. This is why tactical recruitment and dedicated training are so important to your brand.

To come up with a brand promise, consider what customers, employees and partners would expect from every interaction with your staff.

Every business decision should be weighed against this promise to be sure that:

- It fully reflects the promise.
- It does not contradict the promise made.

Staying true to the brand promise, especially in service industries, can be difficult to achieve. The branding strategy is decided by senior management, but the actual brand experience is in the hands of front-line service personnel. These are often the lowest-paid employees and turnover in these jobs can be high. When the employee is not properly trained in what the brand really represents or does not subscribe to the brand values, there is a gap between the customer's expectation and the actual service experience, which leads to customer dissatisfaction. When this is understood, it is easy to see how crucial staff training is to align the brand promise to the customer experience, and yet is very often neglected. No wonder we experience so many service failures in our daily lives.

> ***Example***
> *The Ritz-Carlton Hotels have a clear promise to their customers: "Ladies and gentlemen serving ladies and gentlemen".*

Brand promises can and may change over time. New promises can be added, other promises can be updated, and irrelevant promises can be deleted.

4. Brand Values

Your values are the code by which you will conduct your business dealings to achieve your mission and vision. Again, it is important that your staff know what the organisation's values are so they know how to deliver the promise. If one of your values is to conserve the environment, you would set up office and work environments that support green values such as recycling paper, conserving paper, use of mugs rather than paper cups, etc. If this is a value of the organisation, your staff shouldn't be wasting paper as they go about their work processes.

When a brand claims to be friendly and sincere, every contact point with the customer in every channel must meet that commitment. Translating brand values into the intended experience for the customer means that employees need to fully understand the brand values and promise, and "live the brand".

One important thing to understand here is the psyche of the average customer. Bad service can be devastating to your brand and can cause your customer to switch away from your brand. In organisations that hold a monopoly or near monopoly on the market,

such as telecommunications companies in a lot of countries, the effect of bad service is not so drastically felt because customers can't really go anywhere else, or they feel that the competition is probably just as bad so it is not worth the effort of switching service providers.

However, this is almost certainly not the case in your industry. There are probably a plethora of alternative service providers your customers can switch to if driven to it. Of course this is not to say that monopolistic companies should be apathetic about their standard of service. Even if they don't lose customers, failure to live up to their brand promise will result in integrity lost and a failure to deliver the branded customer experience that today's savvy consumers expect.

Your brand values shown externally will drive your employees' behaviour internally and externally.

Your brand values should be:

- Visible to the public
- Related to your brand promise
- Made to inspire everyone

Example

Let's have a look at the Disney brand again and understand their brand values. Thinking of the Disney values, "happiness" would probably not be your first guess. Not because they don't want their employees or their park goers to be happy; it's that if you teach your employees "happiness" the result for the visitor will not automatically translate to happiness. You have to produce happiness from your core values to get to that end result.

For Disney, the core values are: safety, cleanliness, and superior customer service. If the roller coaster ride is safe, the toilets are clean, and if you get lost and someone helps you, then the end result is happiness.

Now, take a look at an example of how you can communicate your values to your employees using the values of: Accountability, Integrity, Safe & Supportive and Continuous improvements.

WHAT THE VALUE **DOESN'T** MEAN	WHAT THE VALUE **DOES** MEAN
ACCOUNTABILITY	
Blames others or systems when things go wrong, and fails to recognise own part of the problem	Accepts individual responsibility for own actions and overall outcome
INTEGRITY	
Pursues own agenda at the cost of the overall objective, and doesn't appreciate impact of own actions	Takes pride in being proactive, is accurate and attentive to process and detail
SAFE AND SUPPORTIVE	
Shuts down teamwork, and withdraws in difficult situations	Supports decisions and takes responsibility for safety
CONTINUOUS IMPROVEMENT	
Doesn't challenge or raise issues and doesn't listen to feedback	Questions and suggests improvements, open to feedback, and willing to learn

What are your company's values? What do they mean and could they be misinterpreted? Take a few minutes to fill in the table below.

VALUE:	
Doesn't Mean:	**Does Mean:**

VALUE:	
Doesn't Mean:	**Does Mean:**

VALUE:	
Doesn't Mean:	**Does Mean:**

Brand Behaviour

In order to deliver these brand values, your staff need to follow through on Internal Brand behaviours.

Internal Brand behaviours are:

- Visible internally
- Designed to influence how the brand promise is delivered
- Made to inspire everyone

It is the behaviours of your employees that will ultimately deliver your brand promise through an enactment of your brand values. Let's take a look at some examples of value driver behaviours for the retail sector. You can adapt these tables and create your own to train your employees to drive the values for your brand.

Retail Sector Value 1: Convenience	
Behaviours	• We make all our processes convenient and easy to follow. • We can be contacted quickly at any time. • We strive to ensure that the products offered are in stock, but if they are not, we will tell you when we expect more stock. • We ensure we are always available to serve our customers 24/7

Retail Sector Value 2: Passion	
Behaviours	• We ensure that we serve you with delight • We ensure that your every experience with us is memorable through great passionate service • We strive to ensure that we meet your needs and solve your problems with a smile.

ACTIVITY

Now it is your turn again. Fill the table below with your promises and note how your own behaviour and the behaviour of your employees implement these promises.

Value	
List Behaviours	

Value	
List Behaviours	

5. Brand Position

Positioning is how a brand appears in relation to other brands in the market.

This is all about perception. How is your brand perceived by your consumers and employees? Ensuring that your brand is perceived in the same way both inside and out is important to brand building.

Your positioning in the market must be clear to your customers. Have you positioned your brand in the right way?

Example
Here is an example of two brands that are clearly positioned by their price. If Rolex would launch a new product line of cheap watches, it could easily ruin the brand. Conversely, if Wal-Mart were to sell thousand-dollar wristwatches, no one would buy them no matter what their quality. That is why you have to be very careful with your positioning. You would also expect your employees in each of these brands to deliver that positioning to the customers. What would a Rolex front

line employee do that would be different from a Wal Mart employee? For starters it would be just something basic like dress code. While you might find a Wal Mart employee in jeans and a polo tee it is unlikely that a Rolex employee would be dressed that way. You would probably expect the employee of Rolex to be in formal business wear to reflect the positioning of the brand.

Employees need to understand and ensure they consistently communicate your positioning in the market place. If you stand for quality and value, then you need to ensure your employees not just understand your positioning but also deliver it to their customers.

An interesting thing happened to me when I was just starting out in the industry as a young brand executive. I visited a Rolex office to meet with their brand director. Unfortunately, I was late by 10 minutes. The first thing the brand director told me when I walked in was that at Rolex took their time very seriously as they were in the business of time and if I wanted their business I needed to respect their brand and what it stood for. Which meant I needed to be on Time all the Time! It was a powerful lesson for me and has made me respect brands and what they stand for.

6. Brand Personality

Your brand personality communicates your core values and core message, creating an immediate point of differentiation in the marketplace. You need to identify your personality traits and develop a steady persona for your company that does not deviate from these traits. Your personality needs to be consistent and shouldn't change with your audience or message. Remember your personality is going to drive your brand promise, so your audience should not be confused about who you are. If you are environmentally friendly in some outlets and not in others, your customer is not going to be able to pick out clear personality traits that they can identify with your brand. Similarly, if your front-line staff are not delivering your personality at every touch point, you run the risk of not conveying a strong brand personality.

The brand, just like the overall organisation, contains the human characteristics and personality to which customers, consumers and stakeholders relate.

It is the brand personality developed, nurtured and grown by everyone in the organisation that creates that unique and sustainable advantage over other brands – or not.

Kevin Thomson, *Emotional Capital*

As will be described later, Starbucks is a good example of a strong personality, as customers can always expect a well-defined experience each time they walk into a Starbucks café. Other examples of brands that exude personality are products that customers can relate to on an emotional level. Harley Davidson has built up a strong personality following of ardent supporters for its bikes. Customers can associate with the distinctive look, feel and sound of the bikes and can bond as a community. They identify with their fellow riders, even if strangers on the road, recognising that they share a common bond.

Another brand that builds community bonding among its drivers is the VW Beetle. One of their ads captured this sentiment perfectly. Set against a natural disaster occurring in the background, the only thought on one Beetle driver's mind is the sighting of another VW Beetle ahead. "Look there's a yellow one," says the driver, oblivious to the natural disaster happening around him.

Internal DNA

As Organisations develop their brand strategy template we also recommend them to create and internal DNA consisting of the Employee Value Proposition.

Employee Value Proposition:
Employee Value Proposition (EVP) is the commonly used term to describe the characteristics and appeal of working for an organisation.

An EVP describes the mix of characteristics, benefits, and ways of working in an organisation. It is the deal struck between an organisation and employee in return for their contribution and performance. This "deal" characterises an employer and differentiates it from its competition. This essentially means developing a statement of 'why the total work experience at their organisation is superior to that of other organisations.

Example of EVP include:

DuPont:

Creating a World of Possibilities and Opportunities for a Meaningful Life
DuPont brings together people with different talents, aspirations and views to create a highly motivated team that shares the DuPont vision of creating sustainable solutions essential for a better, safer, healthier life for people everywhere.

Creating your Internal DNA

Brand Vision
(where we are headed)

Brand Mission
(why we exist)

Brand Values
(what we stand for)

Brand Personality
(our human attributes)

Brand Positioning
(how we are seen in the marketplace)

Employee Value Proposition
(why we are the employer of choice based on our brand)

Case Study: Ritz-Carlton

The Ritz-Carlton Hotel Company, LLC carries one of the highest brand profiles in luxury lodging and has become a leading brand in the hospitality industry by rigorously adhering to its own standards. To achieve this, they have worked hard to align the internal brand with this high profile external brand, following the Ritz-Carlton motto: "We are ladies and gentlemen serving ladies and gentlemen".

snapshot from www.ritzcarlton.com

The Ritz-Carlton credo is carried out and lived by the employees. The credo states that the Ritz-Carlton is "a place where the genuine care and comfort of our guests is our highest mission. We pledge to provide the finest personal service and facilities for our guests, who will always enjoy a warm, released, yet refined ambience...".

The Ritz-Carlton's long-held belief that employee engagement is linked to customer satisfaction and enhanced profitability goes back as far as the hotel's founder but is still highlighted today. Simon Cooper, who led Ritz-Carlton from 2001 to 2010, explained what makes Ritz-Carlton a brand recognised worldwide:

"We use what we call 'line-up,' which is a Ritz-Carlton tradition. The concept comes from the early restaurants of France, where the chef got his whole team and all the waiters and waitresses and the maitre d' together at 5:30 in the evening. It's a sort of round table. Everybody is there. The chef communicates what they are going to be serving. For the Ritz-Carlton, we want every single hotel, everywhere in the world, every partner, every shift, to utilize line-ups, which typically takes around 15 minutes every day. Part of the line-up everywhere around the world is a "wow story," which means talking about great things that our ladies and gentlemen have done. That is a wonderful training and communication tool, where every department layers on the department message. And it's based on having the same message everywhere, every day, and then each hotel layers on its own message."

"A culture is built on trust. And if leadership doesn't live the values that it requires of the organisation, that is the swiftest way to undermine the culture. No culture sticks if it's not lived at the highest levels of the organisation..."

The Ritz-Carlton has always focused on their service perfection. A 21-day training session in the retention process and 100 hours of additional training every year produces unparalleled guest service. According to Cooper,
"Training is really important, because it nurtures the careers of our ladies and gentlemen. Naturally, in a tough economic climate keeping staff satisfied is more challenging, but obviously it's as important as ever.

"We entrust every single Ritz-Carlton staff member, without approval from their general manager, to spend up to $2,000 on a guest. And that's not per year. It's per incident. When you say up to $2,000, suddenly somebody says, wow, this isn't just about rebating a movie because your room was late, this is a really meaningful amount. It doesn't get used much, but it displays a deep trust in our staff's judgment. Frankly, they could go over that amount, with the general manager's permission".

An amazing branded culture by a world-class brand!

KEY INSIGHT

Key Insights of Chapter 11

- Your vision is how you foresee where your company will be.
- Your mission is the primary purpose of your company's existence - what you set out to do.
- Your values are the code by which you will conduct your business dealings to achieve your mission and vision.
- Your brand promise is what you tell customers you will deliver.
- Positioning is how a product appears as compared to similar brands in the market. For positioning to work, your employees need to communicate your difference.
- Your brand personality communicates your core values and core message, creating an immediate point of differentiation in the marketplace. You need to develop a steady persona that does not deviate from these traits.
- Employee Value Proposition means developing a statement of 'why the total work experience at their organisation is superior to that of other organisations.
- With clear brand strategy, your brand will create a distinction compared to your competitors, thus bringing your brand to the next level.

> The purpose of training is to tighten up the slack, toughen the body, and polish the spirit.
>
> ***Morihei Ueshiba***

Chapter 12

STEP 3: MOTIVATION & INTERNAL TRAINING

1 Brand Research

2 Strategic Blueprint - Brand DNA

3 Motivation and Internal Training

4 Communicate: Delivering the Experience

5 Support Systems

6 Brand Performance Measurement

This is the most crucial stage of your Internal Branding Strategy – putting motivation and training programmes in place to help build your brand credibility, understanding and support internally within your organisation. This is where you finally get the whole organisation on the same page.

WHAT MOTIVATES YOUR EMPLOYEES

Before you can engage in any effective training programme, you need to understand what motivates your employees.

> Fortune magazine's "Most Admired Companies" stock prices appreciated 50% over peers after instituting employee motivation and alignment efforts. All humans have the same basic needs and desires.

Security

An employee needs to feel secure in their job, that it will be there, that they will earn enough to survive the month. Feelings of insecurity can result in the employee resorting to behaviour like theft to compensate.

Variety

People need to be stimulated or they will just be working on autopilot, like a robot, adding no value to the company. Studies show that productivity drops when employees' jobs present no challenge and become boring.

Social Interaction

People need to communicate at work as well as socially. Given the number of hours a day your employees spend at work, this is an innate human trait that you ignore at your peril. If you do not set up your systems to encourage interaction in the workplace, productivity will suffer as employees find other ways to satisfy their need for social interaction which could include making outside phone calls or longer lunch hours.

Value

Your employees, at all levels, need to feel valued and know that their work contributes and makes a difference. You need to ensure that you communicate their value on a regular basis.

Growth

Employees leave organisations in seek of new employment when they feel they can no longer grow with their present organisation. You need to provide avenues for continuous growth for your employees. They must always have a higher goal and feel that it is achievable, yet challenging.

IDEAS TO MOTIVATE YOUR EMPLOYEES TO LIVE YOUR BRAND

Here are some quick ideas to get your employees motivated to Live your Brand. We cover some of these ideas in other chapters but this quick summary will allow you to implement ideas with immediate effect:

How do you get your employees onboard the brand wagon?

Ideas:

- Provide case studies of how brand management has worked in comparable companies and industries.
- Work with HR to integrate a brand-building module into a variety of employee classes.
- Enlist the help of credible outside brand experts to consult with the corporate officer group.
- Hire new high-profile internal brand marketers with a history of success.
- Influence staff with books and speakers about brand and their role in the process.
- Invite senior executives to help you solve brand management problems.

How do you get your employees to act as champions for your brand?

Ideas:

- Ask them for their help in selling the brand. Getting everyone involved, promotes ownership of the brand.
- Ask them, on a regular basis, how the brand management group can help them achieve their objectives, and give them regular feedback in updates in return.
- Communicate how the brand helps their performance targets.
- Educate them on brand power.
- Give them bonuses based on achievement of brand goals.
- Include "brand passion" or alignment of personal brand values to your corporate values as an executive hiring criterion.
- Make them the steering committee for your brand team or internal brand projects.
- Measure the brand's value as an asset. Enlist the support of the CFO and share the news.

How do you keep employees involved and motivated?

Ideas:

- Ask this question on employee surveys: "If you could only change one thing about the brand, what would you change and why?"
- Award staff with brand "certificates of appreciation".
- Capture on videos customer testimonials of how the brand promise was delivered.
- Share them often with employees.
- Catch people "living the brand" and tell stories about them (in newsletters, in speeches, on the company intranet, etc.).
- Conduct "lunch & learn" sessions related to your brand.
- Develop and publish brand performance measures.
- Poster contest ("Communicate what the three brand values mean to you."). Feature twelve of the posters on a 12-month calendar (or 52 of them on a 52 week calendar).
- Have each member of the group share his or her thoughts with others in the group about his favourite brands and why they work.
- Incorporate brand goals in business plans.
- Learn from "best practice" companies. Share information with your peers at other companies.
- On the brand intranet site, post consumer letters highlighting how the brand promise was delivered against (or not).
- Reward a "brand champion of the month".
- Tie performance appraisals and compensation to delivery of the brand promise.

How do you create a brand building culture?

Ideas:

- Develop brand associations and brand stories.
- Lead by example.
- Ask for feedback and get everyone involved to take ownership of the brand.
- Work closely with corporate communications to integrate brand-building education.

How do we communicate the brand through geographically and functionally diverse groups?

Ideas:

- Bring in outside, credible, objective voices who will reinforce your key points – brand executives at other companies, brand consultants, people who are known and trusted by your executive group.
- Build ownership through cross-functional teams.
- Compliment good staff performances.
- Highlight your brand's performance versus the competition (in newsletters, etc.).
- Identify influencers. Create a grassroots support for your initiatives.
- Identify and recruit people in the organisation who "get it" and have passion about the brand.
- Relate your brand programmes back to their issues.
- Sell your initiatives to top executives in other divisions and departments.
- Set up measures to highlight gaps.
- Use networks.
- Widely distribute brand books (books that contain information about your brand).

INTERNAL BRANDING TRAINING – OVERVIEW

Your motivational and training programmes need to take these basic needs into account. You need to get all your employees on the right page before they damage your brand. 90% of employees felt that training was a key factor to learning about the brand but yet many companies do not invest in the right training to build brand awareness and connection.

A successful brand alignment initiative educates employees with the same clear and consistent story.

> For instance, Caterpillar, the global builder of earthmoving equipment and diesel engines, has conducted its One Voice brand education for all its employees around the world since 1993.

Training Model

Specifically, Training should Cover these Key Areas:

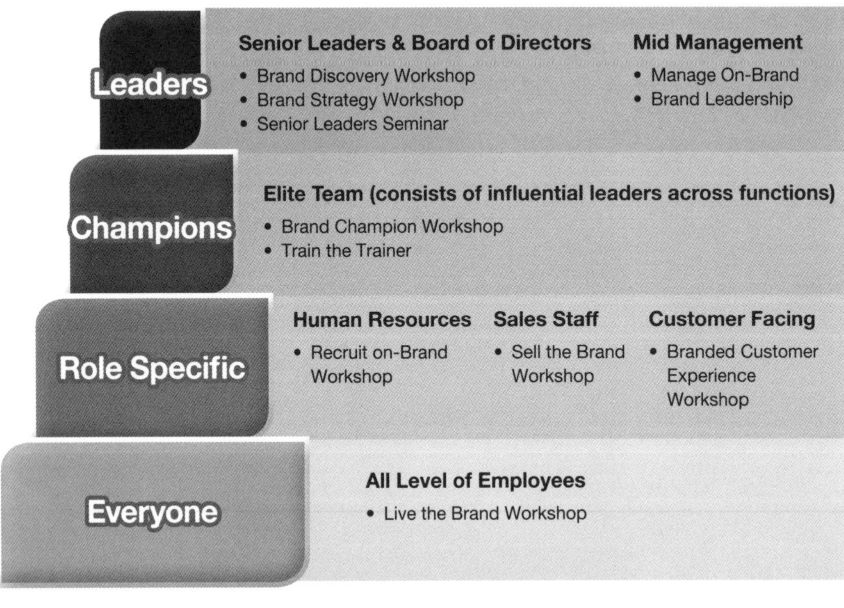

Use this pyramid diagram to develop an internal branding plan that unites and informs all employees with a refreshed brand promise for your organisation.

This will be your plan to articulate and reinforce the brand promise to all employees. This programme will need to engage your employees so that they actively become your brand champions.

WORKSHOPS

Brand Discovery Workshop

This first programme will define for your employees your brand through a series of engaging discovery workshops. The key purpose is to establish your brand before it is launched to the rest of the staff. Discovery workshops are best with Senior Leadership teams to ensure that Leaders are on the same page and in full agreement of the strategic direction of the brand.

Brand Leadership Workshop conducted in Middle East by Brand Coach, Jerome Joseph

Brand Leadership Workshop

For management staff, you will need the following series of workshops:

- A workshop that trains them how to manage on brand so they walk the walk and talk the talk to lead subordinate staff to remain on brand.
- A workshop that trains management staff to empower those they lead so that the brand continues to run through the organisation.

Brand Champions Workshop

This workshop will bring together the top brand champions of the organisation to act as a catalyst to influence the brand from within. Think about this as a knights of a round table. People who defend and act as a guardian for the brand. The role of the workshop is to teach the champions the brand and how they can influence the rest of their colleagues strategically.

Recruit On Brand Workshop

A workshop that trains HR staff and managers on how to recruit on brand. Now that the brand has clearly defined the organisation, this should facilitate recruitment selection, as you should be clear on what kind of people you need to drive your brand.

Branded Customer Experience Workshop

A workshop that trains customer facing staff to translate the brand into an extraordinary customer experience across customer touchpoints. You need to differentiate your customer experience by ensuring it models what your brand stands for. Make employees plot the customer journey and see how you can fit your unique brand experience into that touchpoints.

Sell the Brand Workshop

A workshop that teaches Sales people to focus on their brand so that customer loyalty and differentiation is achieved.

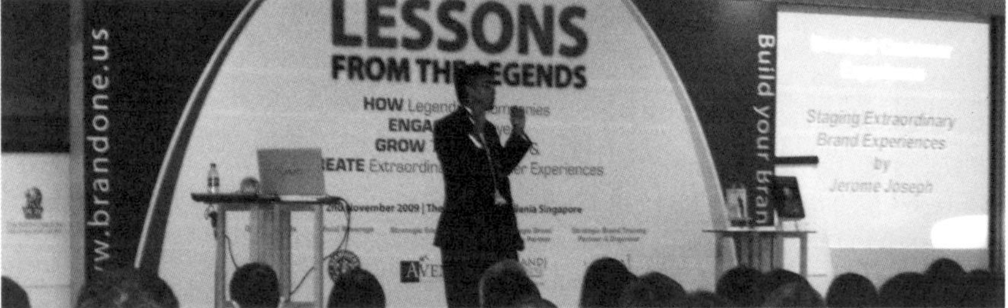

Branded Customer Experience Programme conducted by Brand Coach, Jerome Joseph

Everyone

Live the Brand Workshop

These workshops will take your employees through how to deliver a branded customer experience at each touch point, and another will train on how these brand champions can continue to live the brand in everything they do. This is meant for every body in the organisation.

Live the Brand Workshop conducted for a global consumer IT lifestyle MNC, by Brand Coach, Jerome Joseph

These are just some examples of workshops you can use to build your internal brand.

Properly training employees is important, and it is as equally important to clearly communicate employee expectations, including how they look and behave around clients. Sometimes training falls by the wayside when business owners are busy juggling many tasks at once, but if employees don't understand the image of your brand, the results can be devastating.

I recently called a small business to inquire about their stock. The employee who answered greeted me with "Hello?" He didn't identify himself or the store, making me wonder if I had dialed the wrong number. His attitude didn't communicate interest in the job, and this translated into a lack of interest in doing business on the store's part.

This kind of behaviour reflects badly on the employee, the store, and ultimately, sales. Employees with bad attitudes aren't doing anyone—including themselves—any favours, and one phone inquiry can have a huge impact. I didn't visit the store, and probably won't think of it in the future.

Sample Outline for our ***Live the Brand Workshop***

CLARITY	CONNECTION	CHALLENGES	CHAMPION
YOUR BRAND What does your brand stand for and how would you deliver it?	**BEHAVIOUR** How does your brand behaviour impact your touchpoints?	**OBSTACLES** What are your challenges in creating alignment across your brand?	**LEAD** How can you bring the changes to your peers?
Brand Vision	Touchpoint 1	Product	How do you mentor your colleagues?
Brand Mission	Touchpoint 2	People	How do you be a champion?
Brand Values	Touchpoint 3	Process	What brand stories can you share?
	Touchpoint 4	Policy	

CASE STUDY

Case Study: Starbucks

Starbucks is a good example of what we mean by delivering a strong brand DNA. Customers know, without a shadow of a doubt, what they will experience when walking into a Starbucks café. They will be greeted by friendly vivacious staff. And not only that, staff will endeavour to personalise their conversations with you. This ultimately is the translation of their internal branding built upon expertise, training, quality products and a controlled experience.

Not to mention all those peculiar names for the drinks. Learning the names makes you feel like you're part of an exclusive club – but the price of admission is only a few dollars for an Espresso Macchiato Venti.

Starbucks may offer a diverse mix of coffees and products, but they are always fair trade, they are always created using the best techniques, and employees are continually being trained to evolve them to achieve their highest potential.

"Ultimately Starbucks can't flourish and win customers' hearts without the passionate devotion of our employees. In business, that passion comes from ownership, trust and loyalty. If you undermine any of those, employee will view their work as just another job... their passion and devotion is our number-one competitive advantage. Lose it, and we've lost the game.

Howard Schultz, *Starbucks chairman*

When Starbucks recently shut down all of its 7,000 US stores for a few hours for employee training, they made a powerful statement about how important they think the brand is. The event was, according to a news release, part of the company's ongoing efforts to "renew its focus on the customer." Starbucks' founder, Howard Schultz, said of the idea, "Our unprecedented level of commitment to and investment in our people will provide them with the tools and resources they need to exceed the expectations of our customers."

This was just one initiative from a company that has long demonstrated commitment to helping its employees live the brand. Closing the stores sent an unmistakable message that all 135,000 Starbucks employees are serious about delivering their brand promise.

Key Insights of Chapter 12

- As a foundation, you first need to understand the key elements that motivate your employees: security, variety, social interaction, value, and growth.
- Develop an internal branding plan of workshops and training that unites and informs all employees with a refreshed brand promise.
- Putting these motivations and training programmes in place will help to build your brand credibility, understanding, and support within your organisation.

Chapter 13

STEP 4: COMMUNICATE: DELIVERING THE EXPERIENCE

1 Brand Research
2 Strategic Blueprint - Brand DNA
3 Motivation and Internal Training
4 Communicate: Delivering the Experience
5 Support Systems
6 Brand Performance Measurement

INTERNAL COMMUNICATION FOR YOUR BRAND

In this chapter we will learn how to establish a branded internal engagement programme for delivering the branded experience using engagement, technology, process, and tools.

STRATEGIC BRAND COMMUNICATION TOOLS

Bank Branding from Within

A local Singapore bank division underwent internal changes in a bid to improve internal communication between management and staff. It used its internal staff newsletter as a tool to educate staff about the changes and to involve staff in decision-making processes so that they could truly own the brand. It also held regular dialogue sessions bringing staff of all levels together to suggest ways to improve systems. Staff received acknowledgement in the newsletter if their ideas were implemented. The organisation also organised regular social activities to promote staff bonding and work/life balance. The newsletter proved the ideal tool to successfully communicate the Group's brand direction so that all staff were aware of the brand and their part in its delivery.

Most organisations understand the importance of strategic communication with customers and/or stakeholders, devoting entire departments to the cause. However, few address internal communication in the same way.

Deciding how, when and what to communicate to staff is a chore often performed by managers only when there is a crisis or major event that forces a need for internal communication. However, if they had adopted a consistent approach to internal communication proactively, they wouldn't be scrambling to create one in the advent of a crisis, and they would have a better, more directed and efficient workforce.

The Advantage of Internal Communication

Some of the most successful corporations create a workforce that understands the mission, goals, values and procedures of the organisation. For example, peqple talk about "the Disney way" to describe one organisational culture that is held by trained employees in the organisation. The key of Internal Communication is to enable your staff to understand your brand.

THE INTERNAL COMMUNICATION PLANNING (ICP) PROCESS

Here are the key elements of a successful ICP process:

- **Long-term focus**
  Since the effects of communication exert themselves over an extended period, ICP must be a long-term proactive plan over several years.
- **Clear brand direction**
  First you need to decide the kind of organisation you want, and then plan a communication approach to bring it to life.
- **Broad consistent message**
  You need to take a very broad approach to communication. It is not enough to distribute your vision and mission statements to every staff and hope they see the light. There needs to be consistency of action throughout the organisation from the top down.

How to implement ICP

This depends on the size of your organisation. In a small company, one person may draft the internal communication. In a larger company, there will be more key players. However, no matter the size, the general approach is as follows:

1. Set goals. Answer the question: "What values, principles, procedures and behaviours must we create so that we can achieve our mission?" Set the answers as targets.

2. Pick your tools. You have a wide variety of communication tools at hand to choose from. Select those available to you, and later you will decide which tools will best achieve which goals. Here are just a few ideas:

- **Paper-based:** Memos (internal correspondence), newsletter, brochures, performance appraisal documents, slogans, posters, etc.
- **Oral:** General meetings, division and branch meetings, team addresses, one-on-one (face to face).
- **Electronic:** E-mail, websites and intranets.
- **Management behaviour**: Any and all management/executive behaviour that sends messages, either intentionally or unintentionally about the values, principles, and purpose of the organisation.

- **Staff to management communication:** Surveys, other forums such as staff meetings, individual meetings, etc.
- **Policies & procedures:** Policies and procedures need to be consistent with the messages being sent through other channels.

3. Match tools to goals: Here you match step 1 above with step 2. Some tools are best suited to certain types of goals and not to others. However, be sure you use all tools available to you in some way.

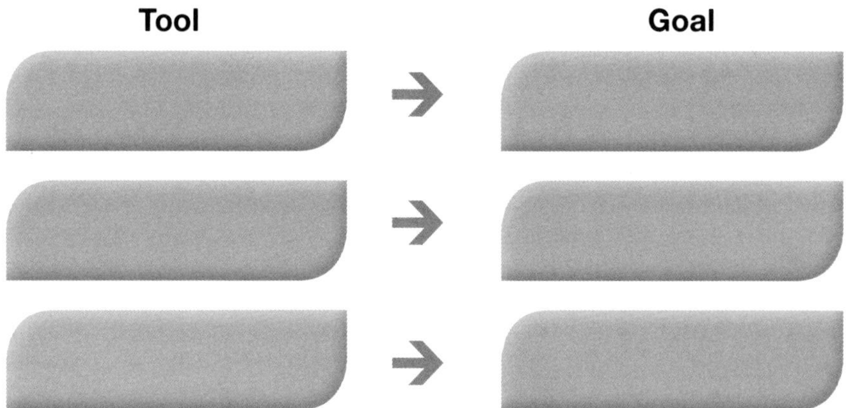

4. Develop a tool blueprint: People using each communication tool need to know both generally and specifically how their tool fits into the larger context. There must be a clear blueprint developed so that all tools are fully maximised and the correct communication message is delivered consistently across the board. Remember to ensure it is aligned to your brand.

5. Plan for skills retraining: You may end up asking people in the organisation to behave and communicate differently so you need to help people develop the skills needed to perform to these new expectations.

6. Set the framework for implementation: Now that you know what you need to communicate and how you are going to do it, you will need to determine who will do what, and when it will be done. This involves all levels of staff and management.
Roll out ICP once all systems are fully in place and everyone understands their role in the entire plan. Then, you are set for success.

7. Continuously review: As technology develops, new communication tools might develop and some tools adopted might become ineffective. You need to continuously monitor all tools to ensure maximum optimisation of use towards your goals.

So, consistent with a continuous improvement approach, we need to assess the effects of what we are doing, and "re-steer" as needed. As suggested in the earlier chapter, use annual internal audits to assess whether progress is being made, and solicit additional ideas.

Tools for internal brand communication

Extracted from Internal Branding: Communicating and measuring the impact by Ramesh Venkat

The workplace today is networked, often virtual and mobile. With this in mind, here are some effective channels for internal brand communication in today's workplace:

- **Corporate portal.** Whether at one's desk or on the road, corporate portals have become a major means for employees to stay connected. The portal can be a gateway to all internal communication. Online publishing is cost-effective, and the content is available 24/7 and is easy to update. Brand toolkits and guidelines can be made available through the portal.

- **Video conferencing.** Philips in India decided that 4,000 employees across diverse business units needed a unified view of the brand. Senior executives set aside a day each quarter to engage in discussions with employees from many locations through video conferencing. Senior management presence, and the interactive nature of the sessions, made this initiative a success.

- **Webcasting**. Webcasts can be recordings of videoconferences made available for viewing anytime, or they can be used to deliver interactive sessions online Unlike traditional video conferencing, employees can sit at their desks and watch or listen to the webcast. Use of presentation tools within webcasts makes this an effective training tool.

- **Podcasts.** Podcasts are audio or video files that are distributed via the Internet on demand. (Video podcasts are sometimes referred to as vodcasts.) Podcasts can be downloaded onto MP3 players or laptops, unlike webcasts, which are streamed via the Internet. Podcasting is effective in communicating brand updates, current news and interviews. Employees can listen to content at anytime from anywhere. In organisations where employees are geographically dispersed, podcasting is an effective way to reach them. BMW's podcasts, for instance, are aimed at customers just as much as at employees. Listeners get to hear what the top executives think of the new products and how brands are positioned in the marketplace. Workers in a BMW factory can get a better sense of how their work is helping the company achieve its business objectives.

- **Blogs.** Corporate blogging is a rapidly growing phenomenon, allowing employees to post opinions about their company, the brand and their own personal experiences with the brand. Unlike other forms of internal communication, blogging allows for the exchange of views, knowledge and experiences and is not a top-down form of communication. If you want your employees to "live the brand," creating a venue where they can share their experiences is important. From General Motors and Ford to Google, Macromedia and IBM, firms are discovering the use of corporate blogging as an effective employee communication tool.

- **Advertising.** Yes, that's right. ING Bank, for instance, took advantage of the fact that their employees visit certain websites, and placed ads on these sites as part of an internal branding campaign aimed at its own employees.

Template for Brand Communication.

Use this template to plan your internal brand communications.

Communication Tools Sample

- PR
- Advertisement
- Name Cards
- Brochure
- Corporate Video
- Sales Letter
- Email
- Presentation
- Postcard
- EDM
- Events
- Social Media
- Website
- E-zine

TOOLS	TARGET AUDIENCE	PURPOSE (Awareness, Promotion, Maintenance)	MESSAGE	TIMELINE
Choose your tools here	Define your target clearly	What is the purpose of this communication?	What is the main mesage of your communication?	When are you going to execute this plan?

Case Study: Google

When was the last time you heard someone talking about "searching the web"? Today we simply say, "I Googled it and found these results." No wonder Google counts as one of the most valuable brands in the world. But what is it about Google? A search engine company whose human resource policies are becoming exemplary? Yes, Google has proven that successful brands are clearly differentiated and Google has done that through its service and through the way they treat its people. The company is a valuable example of strong internal branding, even in the B2B industry. As a result Fortune Magazine has often ranked Google as the number one place to work.

And principles such as "Great just isn't good enough," "Google does search," "Google believes in instant gratification," "You can be serious without a suit," and "The need for information crosses all borders" are just a few they promote.

Google management is very much aware that its success in the market highly depends on having the right people who understand what the Google brand stands for. It doesn't have the typical set of brand values or guiding principles. Instead Google has developed "Ten things Google has found to be true," which simply explains how they operate in the intensely competitive Internet marketplace. The most distinctive factor about Google's internal policies might be that their employees are given considerable freedom within their work scope and everyone is encouraged to innovate on their own. While the founders and CEO remain highly involved, regular employees still have a large impact over the success of the company.

To make sure that freedom and individuality are used to support the company's interests and follow the culture, internal branding efforts are used to foster a culture of innovation and creativity. The work environment for the Google employees in their Googleplexes is following the approach and creates that distinctive environment that you normally won't have in a multinational company. The offices and cafes are designed to encourage interactions between Googlers within and across teams, and to spark conversation about work as well as play. Google strives a lot to maintain this open culture, in which everyone is a hands-on contributor and feels comfortable sharing ideas and opinions, something that normally is associated with small start-ups. In the long run, this will keep the Google model competitive and sustainable.

KEY INSIGHT

Key Insights of Chapter 13

- Internal Communication is critical in communicating your brand to your employees
- Review the cycle constantly to ensure the brand alignment is maintained on an on-going basis.
- Rejuvenate your internal communication with the right tools to reach your audiences.

Chapter 14

STEP 5: SUPPORT SYSTEMS

1 Brand Research

2 Strategic Blueprint - Brand DNA

3 Motivation and Internal Training

4 Communicate: Delivering the Experience

5 Support Systems

6 Brand Performance Measurement

It is critical that your corporate systems revolve around your internal brand. This means that every aspect of your organisation should be aligned and driven to build your internal brand. This include areas such as your KPIs, performance review, reward and recognition, recruitment, mentoring, leadership and many other areas. In this chapter, we are going to focus on some of the important areas, but bear in mind, your entire organisational structure should be driven to support your Brand in every way.

KEY PERFORMANCE INDICATORS

The adage "What gets measured, gets done" is true. KPIs focus employees' attention on the tasks and processes that executives deem most critical to the success of the business. KPIs are like levers that executives can pull to move the organisation in new and different directions. In fact, among all the tools available to executives to change the organisation and move it in a new brand direction, KPIs are perhaps the most powerful.

Subsequently, executives need to treat KPIs with respect. As powerful agents of change, KPIs can drive unparalleled improvements or plunge the organisation into chaos and confusion. If the KPIs do not accurately translate the company's brand strategy and goals into concrete actions on a daily basis, the organisation will flounder. Employees will work at cross purposes, impeding each other's progress, leaving everyone tired and frustrated with little to show for their efforts.

PERFORMANCE REVIEW

As employees, we must deal with employee performance reviews, also referred to as employee appraisals or performance evaluations. Whatever you call them, employee reviews evaluate our performance on the job. They often determine raises, promotions, and sometimes whether we get to keep our jobs.

The key to building your brand from within is to include a strong brand component to your performance review.

RECOGNITION AND REWARD

Employee recognition is a communication tool that reinforces and rewards the most important outcomes people create for your business. 60% of employees indicated that they were not rewarded or recognised for On-Brand Behaviour or for living the brand consistently.

When you recognise people effectively, you reinforce, with your chosen means of recognition, the actions and behaviours you most want to see people repeat.

- All employees must be eligible for the recognition.
- The recognition must supply the employer and employee with specific information about what behaviours or actions are being rewarded and recognised.
- Anyone who then performs at the level or standard stated in the criteria receives the reward.
- The recognition should occur as close to the performance of the actions as possible, so the recognition reinforces behaviour the employer wants to encourage.

A small company working directly with many clients established a criteria for rewarding employees. These included activities such as contributing to the company's success or serving a customer without being asked by a supervisor. Everyone who met the stated criteria received a personal thank-you note by the supervisor, telling exactly why the employee was receiving the recognition.

The note included the opportunity for a little gift from a box. Gifts ranged from fast food restaurant gift certificates and candy to a gold dollar. A duplicate of the thank-you note went into a periodic drawing for even more substantial reward and recognition opportunities.

Imagine you work for a company where the human resources department arranges for every employee to receive a potted plant on the anniversary of his or her hire date. The computer generates a list of employees with upcoming anniversaries, the HR employee then creates the purchase order, and a florist delivers your plant.

When your manager walks by your desk and notices that you have received the standard anniversary plant, she says, "Oh, is it your anniversary?" At that moment, how recognised do you feel? We guess that you feel very good.

Another example was a company we worked with. We worked with them to ensure that their staff were rewarded with a yearly bonus when they met a set of brand milestones.

Rewards and recognition that help both the employer and the employee get what they need from work is a win-win situation. Make sure you plan a recognition process that will "wow" your staff and "wow" you with its positive outcomes.

ACTIVITY

Using this template think of key areas of support in which you can bring your brand into play.

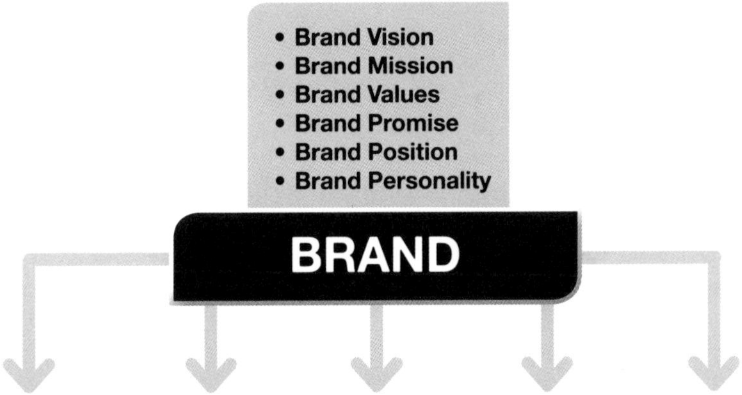

- **Brand Vision**
- **Brand Mission**
- **Brand Values**
- **Brand Promise**
- **Brand Position**
- **Brand Personality**

BRAND

EXAMPLES OF SUPPORT SYSTEMS

BRANDED LEADERSHIP	BRANDED ASSESSMENT	BRANDED RECRUITMENT	BRANDED SOCIAL MEDIA	BRANDED REWARD & RECOGNITION
How do you mentor or lead your staff to live the brand?	How do your KPIs and performance review encourage your staff to live the brand?	Do you have clear hiring guidelines based on your brand?	What are your social media guidelines that will enable your staff to live the brand?	How does your reward and recognition programme encourage staff to live the brand?

CASE STUDY

Case Study: The Virgin Group

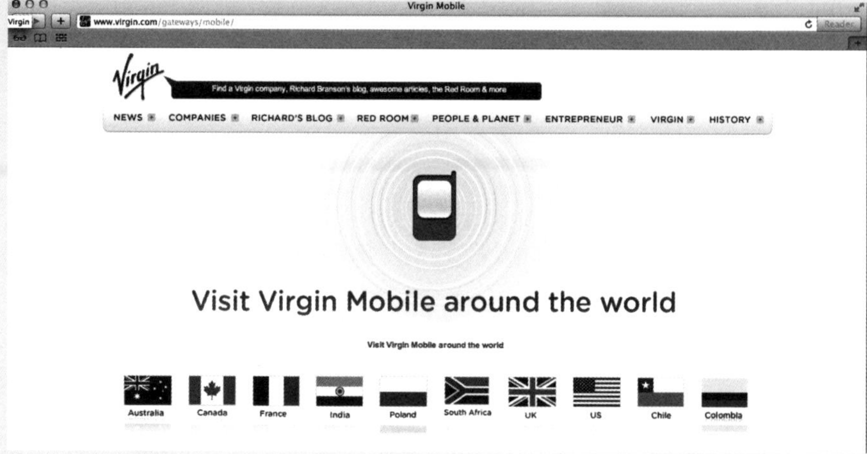

snapshot from www.virgin.com

What is the Virgin Group? Holding over 200 companies privately, this question is not easy to answer. The British multinational branded conglomerate company founded by Richard Branson has extended the Virgin brand to diverse and distinct businesses such as airline, cola, mobile phone, bridal wear, retail chain, financial services, cars, jeans, trains, and books amongst others.

There was quite a lot to unite under the Virgin brand, and as Branson extended Virgin, their human resource management and leadership were facing a huge challenge to align everybody around the brand, maintaining the core brand values.

Today Virgin is well known as an outstanding example of living their brand to the fullest. In an interview, Virgin Mobile's former brand director, James Kydd, gave some insight to the factors that made the brand so resilient. First, he noted, founder Sir Richard Branson has a "long-term vision" fundamentally centred on the idea of "trust and delivering". The combination of a strongly articulated vision and "accountability and responsibility and freedom" among employees in terms of implementing that vision means that the company has enough latitude in terms of executing the brand in different areas.

Virgin is one company that has always recognised the importance of its people. They believe that to create a powerful external brand you need to create a culture that supports it. Generally culture to them is about how the company does business with its staff, as opposed to how it does business with its customers. Unlike other companies, Virgin actively encourages personal expression, creative thinking and expressing your individual style, at least where uniforms are not required. This attitude is also demonstrated in its group brand manual, which starts with "Our People Come First" as the heading for the first chapter.

"We embarked on consciously building Virgin into a brand which stood for quality, value, fun and a sense of challenge. We also developed these ideas in the belief that our first priority should be the people who work for the companies, then the customers, then the shareholders. Because if the staff are motivated then the customers will be happy, and the shareholders will then benefit through the company's success."

Richard Branson
founder Virgin Group

Through putting so much belief and trust into the company's employees, global success rewards Branson every day. The Virgin brand is recognised the world over, and the brand promise is driven consistently over every touchpoint.

KEY INSIGHT

Key Insights of Chapter 14

- Branding is not an isolated practice/campaign. It should be a holistic approach from all aspects of the organisation.

- Creating a system support that based on the brand, will ensure the brand to flourish within an organisation, creating reason for people to believe in the brand and send a signal that you're serious about your brand.

- Ensure your People, Product, Process and Policy works hand in hand across all functions, from hiring to setting KPIs, leadership and reward & recognition.

- Develop an employee recognition tool that reinforces and rewards the most important outcomes people create for your business. Only when you recognise and reward people effectively, they will repeat the actions and behaviours you most want to see.

Chapter 15

STEP 6: BRAND PERFORMANCE MEASUREMENT

1 Brand Research
2 Strategic Blueprint - Brand DNA
3 Motivation and Internal Training
4 Communicate: Delivering the Experience
5 Support Systems
6 Brand Performance Measurement

To foster their ongoing success, the systems you have now successfully put into place will need monitoring on a regular basis. It is through valuable evaluation and feedback that you can keep track of your internal branding effectiveness and ensure your employees remain aligned with your brand. You don't want people skipping pages or reading too slowly and getting left behind. It is crucial to keep everyone on the same page!

MEASURING THE IMPACT OF INTERNAL BRANDING

A recent study by the Canadian Marketing Association (CMA) found that 58 percent of organisations do not measure the impact of their internal branding initiatives. Measurement is a crucial part of ensuring internal-external brand alignment. Here are some tools for measuring the impact of internal branding initiatives:

- **Internal brand equity.** Brand equity is a reflection of the degree of awareness, favourable associations and loyalty that a customer has towards a brand. A similar measure can be established internally. Employee awareness, loyalty and commitment to the brand can be measured through anonymous surveys. Employee actions that are consistent with brand values can be rewarded and tracked, like BP does with its Helios Awards, which recognise teams who "live" the company's brand attributes. Ongoing tracking of brand equity from both customer and employee perspectives will allow firms to address gaps and align brand perceptions.

- **Employee-brand engagement.** The employee-brand engagement survey is a useful tool. A good measure of employee-brand engagement should include feelings (how the employee feels towards the brand, the company and the leadership) and On-brand behaviour (does the employee act and intend to act in ways that are consistent with brand values?).

The success of internal branding depends on the message, the medium and measurement. Choose media that are engaging, interactive and emotionally appealing. As with any business activity, measure the impact of internal brand communication. What gets measured really does get done.

BRAND METRICS

The use of new communication tools becomes more relevant and old tools become obsolete over time. As improvements are continuous, we need to assess and adjust what we are doing as needed. This can be through annual surveys on progress or additional ideas for improvement. Develop a set of internal brand tracking metrics. Set requirements for the research that cover the brand programme both internally and externally.

To keep track of your successes and failures, you must measure your internal brand performance. While being able to celebrate successes with your teammates, you will also be able to promise to move things back on track during a downturn or after a failed project, because you will now understand how things work.

Brand metrics help companies strategically grow their brands internally by:

- Providing criteria to push them through a process.
- Providing a holistic understanding of how the brand is performing.
- Helping sustain communications and organisational devotion.
- Helping to effectively delegate resources on an on-going basis.

With today's technology, measuring your performance is easier, cheaper and quicker.

BRAND SCORECARD

Having gone through the process of developing a set of brand metrics, it is useful for a company to develop a brand scorecard. This synthesises all of the selected metrics into one visual tool, which then serves as a dashboard to manage the brand. The company is then able to quickly identify trouble spots and take action to correct the problem.

An effective brand scorecard.
A brand scorecard must have these metrics. The advantages of these metrics include making it easy to collect data and measure its relevance to profitability growth. Equally as important, the rest of the organisation can easily understand them.

Customer retention and lifetime.
Customer retention and lifetime can be correlated with employee performance and satisfaction to see if employee satisfaction results in increased customer satisfaction.
Internal Brand penetration: Measures how well the brand is projected by the employee/ touchpoints.

Customer loyalty.
Many different indicators can be used here but the most common is the number of referrals. Does customer loyalty correlate to employee loyalty?

Brand metrics help management recognise areas that need to be improved and take the appropriate steps to getting back on track. With a right set of metrics, an organisation can focus on brand growth, use a strategic plan to measure the brand's performance growth, and allocate resources for short and long-term business impact. When the brand is performing at its optimum, the company will learn that the organisation is holistically healthier and delivers more to the bottom line.

Using this template think of key areas of measurement in which you can score for your brand.

Attributes	Baseline Pre Initiative	Goal	Actual Post Initiative	% of Goal	Value Score
A. Brand State					
Brand Awareness - External					
Brand Perception - External					
Brand Awareness - Internal					
Brand Perception - Internal					
Overall Brand Strength					
B. Employee Brand Performance					
Employee Loyalty					
Employee Engagement Level					
Employee Alignment					
C. Customer & Business Performance					
Customer Loyalty					
Customer Satisfaction					
Revenue per Customer					
Churn Rate					
Business Revenue					

CASE STUDY

Case Study: IBM

A while ago IBM re-engineered their internal structure, aligning their marketing, communications and corporate social responsibility departments closer together. Not because the company needed greater efficiency or synergy between these but because they felt the world in which they operated had changed. In response to this newly connected global community of experts and chatters, IBM merged branding and culture into a new management discipline.

Jon Iwata, the senior vice president of communication and marketing at IBM, spoke about this in his speech "Toward a New Profession: Brand, Constituency and Eminence on the Global Commons":

"I believe the most powerful advantage of putting these teams [of marketing, communications and CSR] together is that we have combined our culture with our brand, and our values are the foundation of both... The integration of marketing, communications and CSR is not only logical, it is inevitable – because of all the changes in the external environment – the need to speak with one voice across advertising, sales promotion, events, websites, the media, analysts, bloggers and the like."

As he continued he went into detail about why IBM had created this new internal discipline that combined brand management and what he called "workforce enablement," aligning "experts in the workplace and experts in the marketplace."

The underling reason is that "one day soon, every employee, every retiree, every customer, every business partner, every investor and every neighbour associated with every company will be able to share an opinion about that company with everyone in the world, based on first hand experience. The only way we can be comfortable in that world is if every employee of the company is truly grounded in what their company values and stands for."

In anticipation, Jon emphasized the need to "go from managing outward expressions and manifestations of the company...to the behaviour and performance of people."

The second aspect he talked about was the need to create constituency. "In the circle of this room, we talk about constituents all the time. We talk about stakeholders, audiences and agendas. Certainly, I mean the 'creation of constituency' in this way. But the building of constituency goes beyond the reaching of audiences. It gets to how a company establishes shared attraction and shared values: how it shapes not just common ground, but a deeper, enduring, shared idea."

His third and last dimension of the new profession is then building the eminence of the workforce:

"What will determine success or failure in the coming era will be not whether your people show up on the global commons, but what they do once they're there. The key, in other words, is to build the eminence of our workforce. What do I mean by 'eminence'? No matter what their industry, their profession, their discipline or their job, people with eminence are acknowledged by others as expert. It's not simply to know a lot about Tuscan villas, digital cameras or banking. You need to be recognised as an expert.... Because being an expert and being good at communications aren't the same thing, as we all know. Which is why we need to make the creation of this kind of workforce an intentional act, a new discipline in our function. Yes, we need guidelines and policy – but also training, resources and support for broad networks of experts."

Source: Speech delivered on the future of the communications profession at the November 4th 2009 Institute for Public Relations Distinguished Lecture Series at the Yale Club in New York City.

Key Insights of Chapter 15

- Systems you have successfully put into place will need monitoring on a regular basis.
- Develop a set of brand tracking metrics, which will help you strategically grow your brands but be careful because they are not as easy as they sound. The right brand metrics will help management to recognise areas that need to be improved and take the appropriate steps to getting back on track.
- Create your brand scorecard that synthesises all of the selected metrics into one visual tool, which then serves as a dashboard to manage the brand.

BONUS CHAPTER: GOING THE EXTRA MILE

Chapter 16:

CREATING THE BRANDED CULTURE

Culture is an important aspect of brand building from within. Once the internal branding initiative kicks off. It would be wonderful to sustain it through a culture driven by your brand.

Tony Hsieh is the founder and CEO of the online shoe and clothing shop Zappos.com. He is a big advocate of culture and goes on to say this in his blog:

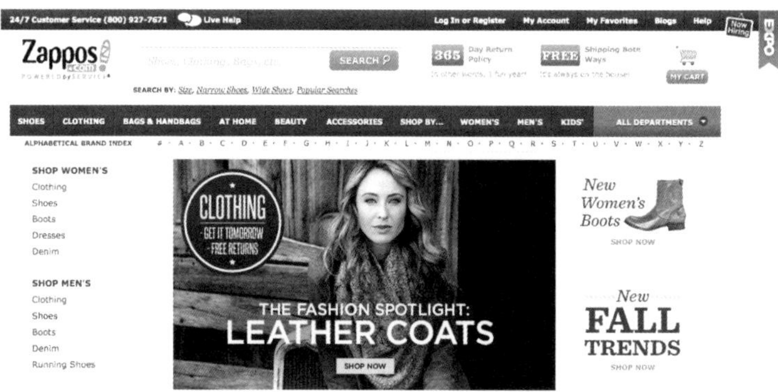

snapshot from www.zappos.com

"At Zappos, our belief is that if you get the culture right, most of the other stuff — like great customer service, or building a great long-term brand, or passionate employees and customers — will happen naturally on its own.

We believe that your company's culture and your company's brand are really just two sides of the same coin. The brand may lag the culture at first, but eventually it will catch up.

Your culture is your brand."

Zappos is not the only organisation big on culture. In our Internal brand survey 50% of organisations have invested building a culture. 80% of executives recognise the need to align brand to the their culture but only 20% are doing so.

The key is that once you have developed your internal brand it has to become more than just words. It has to be a Way of Life for your organisation.

ADVANTAGES & BENEFITS OF A COMMON CULTURE

Companies create cultures to set common goals on which employees can act every day. This brings a coherence to the workplace and empowers employees to act and make decisions within given parameters.

A strong common culture:

- Empowers employees to make more decisions themselves and reduces the need to micromanage.
- Encourages staff to make a difference by giving them a sense of identification with or ownership of the brand. This increases effort and efficiency.
- Fosters the sharing of a common vision and purpose, which will reduce day-to-day conflicts.
- Helps staff feel where they belong.

Once the benefits are understood, a company needs to harness all of its organisation's communication resources in order to adopt a common culture effectively.
Consistency is the key. Successful companies use multiple methods of internal communication, consistently, from training to written communication to management behaviour. Simply put, internal communication won't happen on its own. It needs to be effectively and meticulously planned in order to bring all employees onto the same page.

CREATING A BRANDED CULTURE THROUGH BRAND ASSOCIATIONS

There are many cases of brands that are so easily recognised by a sound, a symbol, a hero, or an object that the public doesn't have to see the name to know what brand it is associated with.

What companies need to do is to develop a list of associations for their brand and ensure that its communicated not just to their customers but also to their employees. Some companies excel at creating associations. For example, one of the companies that we did internal branding work for, was a sports management company with a strong culture based on a common love for soccer. So we created soccer associations to drive this culture. The CEO was called Gafer and staff were called Players. Every month they had team meetings where we encouraged them to use words such as "Go for Goal" and "Score to Win". Other things they did was also to ensure that life size soccer balls were placed around the office with inspirational sporting quotes from soccer stars.

Here are some associations that you can create when you develop your Internal Culture:

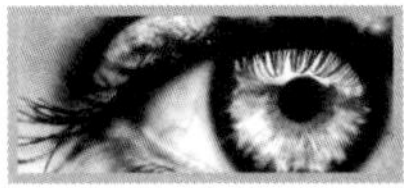

1. Sight: Do you have pictures or visual cues which represent what your brand is about? Is this placed around your office? When ABNB Federal Credit Union launched their new brand identity, they held a special employee pep rally to explain the change and inspire employees – including elements such as a skit and guitar performance by Vice Presidents.

2. Smell: Have you been to an Abercrombie store? If yes, you might even now have a sense of the typical strong Abercrombie smell that is part of the unique experience at any of their stores. (One would assume that the staff of Abercrombie could also have a signature smell?) Are there certain smells you can own?

3. Touch: One of our clients had a logo that looked like a red brick and a brand that stood for security. As a result we created a brick wall in the middle of their canteen, which employees could write on and touch to reinforce what their brand stood for. At the end of the month we photographed the wall and placed another new wall. The photographs were all displayed so that employees could take pride with what they had written.

4. Taste: What authentic taste can you make your own? For a brand that we worked with, their values formed an acronym "CREAM" (Care, Responsible, Efficient, Attentive and Motivate) as a result once a month we created " Ice Cream" day where staff had to bring Ice Cream for a fellow colleague and share a story related to any of the values.

5. Sound: Just think of the sound heard when a PC laptop is started up - unmistakably Microsoft – you don't have to lift your head from your newspaper to check – it is globally recognised from the sound alone. What sound or even music can you make your own. We recently met a Non profit organisation whose signature song was "Don't Stop Believing" by Journey, which was linked to their vision of Believe. The song was played at all staff events and even on their phone waiting system.

6. Symbol: The Nike symbol is recognised the world over without any need for the name to be visible. Symbols are a powerful way to trigger the mind to what a brand stands for. What kind of symbols can you use to depict what your brand stands for internally? For example when we worked with an international airport on their internal brand, we created a mascot for them to symbolise their brand values. Once a month Mr Mascot would go around the airport giving away goodies and also reminding staff of their brand.

7. Hero: A brand can be associated with a hero figure. Pepsi took the Coke/Pepsi war a step further when it signed a series of popular celebrities, including Britney Spears. Suddenly it was hip to drink Pepsi. Omega watches enlists celebrities who speak to their brand image, including Bono, Cindy Crawford, and Brad Pitt. From an internal perspective, heroes come in all shapes and sizes. You have heroes such as Steve Jobs of Apple and Bill Gates of Microsoft. Create heroes in your organisation that can reflect what your brand stands for. This would include people such as your leaders or that everyday staff that showcases an extraordinary passion to your brand.

8. Rituals: Rituals are collective activities, considered socially essential within a culture. Examples include ways of greeting, ways of paying respects to others and social and religious ceremonies or coffee cultures.

Rituals create affinity towards a brand and provide us with a reason, consciously or unconsciously, to revisit the brand experience. It imparts something personal that brings us closer to the brand. Building a ritual is as distinct as the offering, but there are two rules that need to be adhered to.

- Firstly, there must be consistency. If the ritual is not always present then it becomes an ad hoc experience more likely to create disappointment by its omission than satisfaction by its inclusion.
- Secondly, it must be meaningful. If the rituals aren't meaningful they are not going to become personal, and a successful ritual needs to trigger and maintain a personal relationship.

The Ritz-Carlton Line-up

A powerful ritual is that of the Ritz Carlton Line up. The Ritz-Carlton is not alone in creating rules or guidelines to keep employees focused on the company's values and mission, but the Ritz-Carlton does stand apart in how it reinforces those values with every employee, every day.

Each day at every Ritz-Carlton around the world, employees from every department gather for a 15-minute meeting, known as a "line-up," to review guest experiences, resolve issues, and discuss ways to improve service. These line-ups are unlike most meetings held on any given day in most corporations. Once basic housekeeping items are out of the way, most of the rest of the time is spent reinforcing one of the 12 service values. Telling Wow Stories have the power to inspire, motivate, and reinforce a company's culture, vision, and values. During the line-up, someone reads what is known as the "wow story" of the day. The same story is shared across hotels in 21 countries, so a waiter in Boston will hear the same story as a concierge in Jakarta; a housekeeper in Shanghai will hear the same story as a doorman in Hong Kong. The stories single out a staff person who went above and beyond—offering exemplary service to help create the mystique that turns luxury travellers into repeat guests.

9. Props: Company X is a brand about fun and experiences. They sell video editing systems found in phones so you can edit your home videos. In their office they have a playground with a mock setting of the beach for their staff to relax and have fun. They also have a pantry with a 60s rock and roll theme. Their meetings take place in a mock theatre setting. All these props reinforce the idea of the brand and what it stands for.

The key to creating an internal culture is really a combination of all of the above, it takes work to create your internal brand strategy and cultivate a strong internal culture, but the payoff is worth the time and effort invested when you get it right.

A Harvard Business School study conducted over 11 years showed a variety of areas in which companies with the right brand culture outperformed their counterparts. Revenues were 4.1 times higher, stock prices were 12.2 times higher, and return on investment was 15 times higher.*

It's hard for businesses to be consistent internally or externally if they haven't fully defined who they are and how they want to evolve. Find what makes your organisation unique, cultivate it, celebrate it and culturalise it. Help your employees understand your business's unique story and make it their own.

ACTIVITY

Develop your own brand associations through our template. Think of your mission, vision and values and linked them to the different associations.

Association	Vision	Mission	Value 1	Value 2	Value 3
	What is your vision	What is your mission	What is your value	What is your value	What is your value
Sight					
Smell					
Touch					
Taste					
Sound					
Symbol					
Hero					
Rituals					
Props					

YOUR BRAND STORY

A big part of brand culture is to create a vault of stories to drive your brand. Your first question is probably, "What the heck is a brand story?"

Your brand story is literally this: the story of how your company got started and why it exists today. It could even be about your customers, your achievements, your brand values and so on. Every good story has a problem, and a narration of how that problem was solved.

Your story must consist of a concise story line. Start with a situation and a problem to be resolved.

Look at the oldest stories of history. There is almost always a hero. Everybody loves a hero. In your story, your company is the hero.

Say you own a software company. In your story, you relate that once upon a time there was no easy-to-use application for finding your favourite music online. So your company was founded to fulfil this unmet need. Now, thanks to your company, millions of people around the world can easily find the music they like.

Your brand story is a key part of your overall branding strategy. It must be carefully developed over time, tested, and refined until it is perfect. Best of all, if it is told to your employees, they can better relate to the brand and in turn share these stories.

Your brand story is the ideal tool to unite your staff in a common purpose within your organisation. It allows them to connect with the people they serve on the outside. Telling them these brand stories gives meaning to who you are and what you do.

Far from being a cocktail reception speech, your brand story is your key business driver. The more coherent and compelling your brand story, the more it will power the success of your company. But it's got to be carefully planned to be done correctly.

An IBM story

Many years ago, so the story goes, a security guard stopped IBM CEO Thomas Watson, Jr., as he was about to enter a secure area without his identification badge. Watson explained who he was, but the guard insisted that a badge must be worn in restricted areas of the building. Rather than discipline the guard, Watson praised him and used this experience to tell others about performing their job well.

Stories and legends like this about past corporate incidents serve as powerful social prescriptions of the way things should (or should not) be done. They provide human realism to individual performance standards and use role models to demonstrate that organisational values are both enduring and attainable.

Here are some tips to making your brand story as effective as it can be when you're speaking to prospective customers.

Make it clear

As we mentioned before, if you aren't clear about what you do, your prospect isn't going to be either. You need to plan your story so that it tells your listener succinctly and clearly what it is that you do, and why and how the listener can benefit.

Be consistent

Build a core vocabulary that tells your story and stick to it whenever and wherever you deliver your speech. Ensure that this vocabulary is carried through all your marketing collaterals. This creates unity and consistency, and helps to build your brand.

Add a little pizzazz

This will help you connect with the listener on an emotional level and help keep their attention. Everyone likes to be entertained. With the emotional connection, people are more likely to want to buy from you as opposed to from your competitors.

Keep these points in mind as you prepare your story, as these are absolutely essential elements to a strong brand story. And as you write, be aware that everyone loves a good story. A good story will stay in the minds of your audience. However, to achieve this you need your story to be memorable. It needs to express the core values of your organisation and answer the questions:

- Why do your customers need you?
- Why are you the one to deliver to those needs?
- Why would your customer choose you above all others?

If your brand story doesn't address these issues, you are not saying anything to your audience.

When you hear a good brand story, it often seems to effortlessly trip off the tongue. But if you have tried to craft your own brand story, you will probably have realised that it takes a lot of forethought, meticulous planning and attention to the message and the vocabulary of the brand for you to hit the mark.

BUILDING BRAND STORIES

To build effective brand stories for your organisation, you need the input of others. Encourage managers to share their stories for dissemination through the organisation. Choose from these stories when you need to deliver a brand story to appeal to a particular audience. Which story will resonate best?

- Run a contest for all employees so that you'll hear their stories too.
- What stories do you keep coming back to? Which can you use on a day-to-day basis to explain your brand in a memorable entertaining and impactful way?

Go ahead and define and craft your brand story. Expect it to take days, weeks or even months. Give it the time it deserves and you will have a story that people will remember.

IMPACT OF A GREAT BRAND STORY

Now that we have briefly covered the essentials of crafting a brand story, we will take it to a greater depth to get across the difference of impact a well-crafted brand story can make and how it can be used as a communication tool internally within the organisation to propagate the brand message among your staff and have everyone living the brand.

Use your brand story at every chance to propel awareness, consideration and buying of your brand by the prospects that you meet. Your brand story is not mere window dressing. It is the key to empowering the success of your brand, if it is crafted correctly.

Compare these two brand stories:

Story A

Story A talks about the leadership of CEO John Adams of Company ABC and his achievements to date.

Story B

Story B talks about the challenges and how CEO John Adams overcame those challenges with a clear plan and went on to build a successful company.

Story A is a professional, clear account. But Story B will have everyone's attention and links back to the fact that you can overcome all challenges if you set your mind to it. Think about it. Stories you've heard over the years from mentors will have stayed with you longer than information you have read in training manuals. Why is this so? A story appeals to both sides of the brain – the functional and rational aspects of the left brain and the emotional aspects of the right brain. Is your brand story lacking the emotional appeal?

Work on connecting with your audience's emotions and you will have a much more powerful brand story to tell.

Easier communication of your brand to and for staff

You can also use your brand story to communicate the brand effectively to your staff across all departments and levels. This works because:

- Stories lead by example. They provide the model for communication that your employees can adopt.
- Stories inspire employees to succeed by the inspiring stories they hear.

So how do you make your brand story resonate with your employees? How do you inspire? This is done by taking care to use location appropriately, taking the correct action, and showing the results that evoke an emotional response.

Situation

The situation you place your story in must be significant to your brand and it must be specific. Don't generalise (there was a man who...). Give real names and make the story plausible. (My last manager John Ng said...).

Action

When describing the action taken to address the situation mentioned, make sure they are relevant to your audience. Talk to your employees on their level and appeal to their emotions so that they can empathise and relate.

Results

The outcome of your story must be a result that is realistic and will resonate with your employees. It should appeal emotionally so your employees can connect with the brand.

Using our template, List stories that you can use to build your brand culture:

TARGET AUDIENCE	BRAND HISTORY STORIES	CUSTOMER SUCCESS STORIES	LEADER SUCCESS STORIES
Who are your target audiences? What do you want to convey with this particular audience?	How does the brand history resonate with this particular audience? Situation, Action, Result	How does a customer success story resonate with this particular audience? Situation, Action, Result	How does a leader success story resonate with this particular audience? Situation, Action, Result

CASE STUDY

Case Study: The Zappos Experience

Tony Hsieh is the founder and CEO of the online shoe and clothing shop Zappos.com.

The pizza story told by him is a classic example of brand story that best demonstrates the brand.

This story has become a part of the Zappos narrative. This story has been told by Tony hundreds of times. It brilliantly demonstrates to what lengths Zappos will go to serve their customers. And each time he tells it, Tony says that he hesitates to share it because he doesn't want people to call his company to order pizza.

Here's the story (excepted from his book, Delivering Happiness, at the Huffington Post):

"I'm reminded of a time when I was in Santa Monica, California, a few years ago at a Skechers sales conference. After a long night of bar-hopping, a small group of us headed up to someone's hotel room to order some food. My friend from Skechers tried to order a pepperoni pizza from the room-service menu, but was disappointed to learn that the hotel we were staying at did not deliver hot food after 11:00pm. We had missed the deadline by several hours.

In our inebriated state, a few of us cajoled her into calling Zappos to try to order a pizza. She took us up on our dare, turned on the speakerphone, and explained to the (very) patient Zappos rep that she was staying in a Santa Monica hotel and really craving a pepperoni pizza, that room service was no longer delivering hot food, and that she wanted to know if there was anything Zappos could do to help.

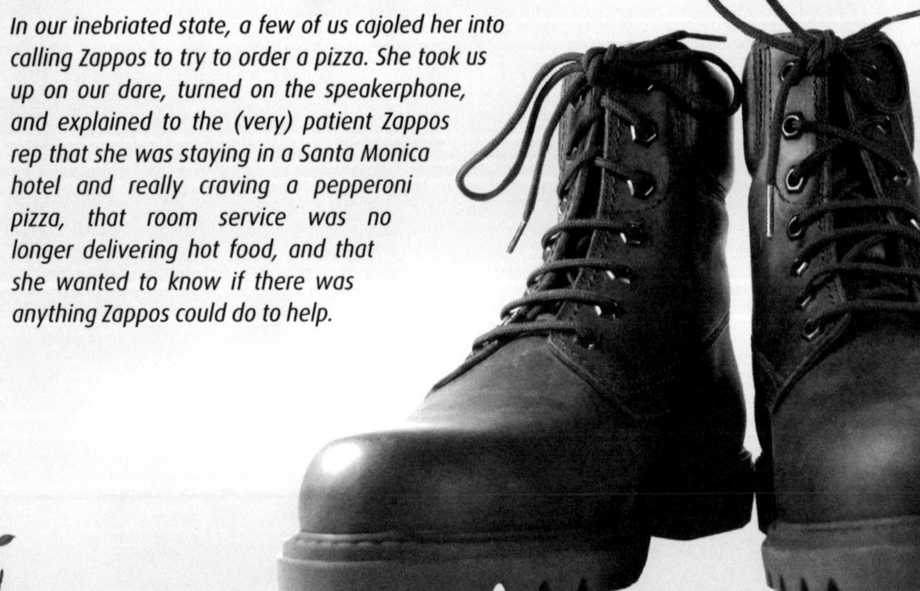

The Zappos rep was initially a bit confused by the request, but she quickly recovered and put us on hold. She returned two minutes later, listing the five closest places in the Santa Monica area that were still open and delivering pizzas at that time.

Now, truth be told, I was a little hesitant to include this story because I don't actually want everyone who reads this book to start calling Zappos and ordering pizza. But I just think it's a fun story to illustrate the power of not having scripts in your call centre and empowering your employees to do what's right for your brand, no matter how unusual or bizarre the situation. As for my friend from Skechers? After that phone call, she's now a customer for life."

Tony could have said, "Our service is the best," or "We'll do anything for our customers." But by telling this story he doesn't have to. Instead, he shares an experience that a listener can relate to. And we draw our own conclusions.

What stories are you giving your customers to tell?

Excerpt Taken from his book, Delivering Happiness, at the Huffington Post
Shared online by Brand Story Blog

Key Insights of Chapter 16

- Create a culture driven by your Brand.
- Use the power of brand associations like, a sound, a symbol, a hero or an object that are so easily recognised to drive Brand Connection. Strong brands never happen by accident. So prepare your success with a sophisticated Brand association strategy.
- Your brand story is the ideal tool to unite your staff in a common purpose within your organisation and it allows them to connect with the people they serve on the outside.
- The story needs to express the core brand values of your organisation and answer these questions: Why do your customers need you? And why are you the one to deliver to those needs?
- You can also use your brand story to communicate the brand effectively to your staff across all departments. They provide the model for communication that your employees can adopt and inspire employees to succeed by the success stories they hear.

THE BEGINNING

> "Authenticity is the alignment of head, mouth, heart, and feet – thinking, saying, feeling, and doing the same thing – consistently. This builds trust, and followers love leaders they can trust."

Lance Secretan,
British leadership theorist

I hope that you have enjoyed the journey through the world of internal branding. Together, we looked behind the walls of some of the most successful brands in the world and learned from their branding initiatives.

We discovered how to build a strong internal brand that will impact your bottom line over the long term. You learned what and how to tell your staff about brand commitment. You learned how to explain it, and you learned how to align and motivate everyone in your organisation.

Above all, you learned the importance of an outstanding brand and how this can impact both your employee and overall brand experience. .

In the first part, some of the strategies for internal branding include, articulating your brand promises to your employees, supporting your growth strategy, defining your brand experience for your employees so they can deliver it, and defining your reputation as a place to work. Why you need to keep your promises and why your employees have such a big impact on your overall success was one of the key points we shared with your with earlier chapters.

In the second part, we focused on what internal branding is about: internal branding builds – through your employees - the bridge between business strategy and implementation. Five essential key steps, the 5 Cs, have been identified to succeed an internal branding effort: CLARITY, CONNECTION, COMMITMENT, CONSISTENCY & CHAMPIONING.

Then, in the third part, we talked about the How. We introduced the Internal Brand Strategy Action Plan (IBSA) and explained to you step by step how you will get your employees aligned and a strong internal brand implemented. Starting with research, strategic blueprint to delivery, motivation, recognition and finally measurement of your success!

In a special bonus chapter, we shared the key to creating a branded culture for your organisation through Brand Associations and Brand Stories.

Thank you for coming with us on this journey to grow your brand from within. Internal branding remains one of the most overlooked areas in businesses around the world and if implemented effectively can be a powerful strategy for growing your brand. We hope this book is just the begining to growing and cultivating your brand from within.

For more information I invite you to contact me at: Jerome@jeromejoseph.com to learn how we can help you in this alignment process.

Let the Journey Begin!